Love
in translation
LETTERS TO MY
COSTA RICAN
DAUGHTER

Katherine
Stanley
Obando

Illustrated by
Priscilla Aguirre

972.86
178g   Stanley, Katherine
        Love in Translation: Letters to my Costa Rican
        Daughter / Katherine Stanley. - 1 ed. -San José,
        CR. :
      K. Stanley, 2016
        164 p. ; 13x20 cm.

        ISBN-13: 978-0692809440

        1. Personal Stories. 2. Essays. I. Title.

For further contact information, visit www.ticotimes.net.

Excerpts from this book first appeared in *The Tico Times*, *The Huffington Post* and the
personal blog *The Dictionary of You*.

ISBN-13: 978-0692809440

First published 2016
Published simultaneously in the United States of America and Costa Rica
Printed in Costa Rica by Litografía e Imprenta LIL, S.A.

Cover art by Priscilla Aguirre
Book design by Andrés Madrigal

10 9 8 7 6 5 4 3 2 1

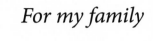

For my family

CONTENTS

INTRODUCTION

To raise a child in someone else's country is a strange proposition. It means relishing or rejecting, depending on the day, a culture that will never be quite your own, while knowing that your child will understand it instinctively and take it for granted. It means accepting that you will never stop learning the language around you, a pianist plunking out "Chopsticks," while your toddler is already playing Bach by heart. It means missing strange things from home at random moments—say, late-summer light through a bottle of worn sea glass on your grandmother's kitchen windowsill—and then realizing that your child may never miss those things at all.

All of us know this loneliness, of course. No one lives the same life as his or her parents. All mothers and fathers, sons and daughters, yearn to be understood. In a multicultural family, this basic truth is simply accentuated. We know right up front that there is much space between us, much to explain. As I look at my daughter and think about that sea glass, that is what I feel: the need to explain.

I also feel the need to preserve. My U.S. past is distant, but my Costa Rican present seems to be slipping through my fingers as well. We live at the edge of one of the last urban coffee fields in the capital. Like the tiny building gradually swallowed up by the city in one of my favorite childhood books, Virginia Lee Burton's *The Little House*, the field we love is a confused little scrap of wind-rustled leaves, wondering what happened to the mile after dark green mile that once surrounded it. It is now hemmed in on all sides by housing complexes but used to stretch nearly all the way to my husband's childhood home, eight kilometers or so to the east, where only thirty-odd years ago he walked on dirt roads and played among the coffee plants. Now those roads are paved. The places where he played are filled with buildings. Children stay inside, dazzled by touch screens.

Today, I walk with my daughter by that stubborn little coffee field and wonder how long it will last. Her presence makes me realize that it is all fleeting: the field, the street-vendor calls that punctuate our days and rattle our windows, the New Englander who walks these warm hills with snow in her bones. I worry that no one will tell her about these things— about the time and people and place that brought her about—if her dad and I are hit by the proverbial bus. Or an actual bus, which is entirely possible in a city where bus drivers are pretty much exempt from any traffic laws whatsoever, and alternate between glacial slowness and the joyful, highly lethal cutting of corners, the latter usually in the rainy dark for maximum danger. But I digress.

One of my favorite parts of my daughter's homeland is also one of the most malleable: its language, particularly its street vernacular, which is unstable by definition. While people who visit my adopted country might love many different things about it—its empty beaches, its lack of an army, the way its cold beer tastes with ice, salt, and lime—what I love the most about Costa Rica is the way it talks. I love the poetry of its slang, so specific and complex that it can vary from one small neighborhood to the next, just like San José's quirky microclimates. I love its endless repertoire of *dichos*, the folk sayings that are always at the ready on the tongues of my coworkers and friends to bemuse, reassure, or instruct me. I love the way that anyone, from a taxi driver to a president, takes pride and pleasure in being the first to initiate a wide-eyed foreigner into a new turn of phrase, the way I imagine a Frenchman might unveil a cherished wine or an Italian her mother's finest dish.

As my years in Costa Rica have ticked by and my initial infatuation with the country has been replaced by a more nuanced understanding of its considerable warts and flaws, this nation's love for a good play on words has remained a bright spot on the darkest day. Without any doubt, the way Costa Rica speaks—and thinks—

has changed my life. And my affair with Costa Rican language went from a spirited fling to a lifelong commitment when, after a few years as a reporter wandering through the country's press conferences, protests, and *precarios*, I married one Costa Rican and gave birth to another.

So as a new mother looking back on my first decade in this country, trying to honor my little U.S.-Costa Rican daughter who will find her own ways to digest the strange soup of language and culture she's being fed, I decided to write her a dictionary of sorts. As she pores over books instructing her that "a" is for apple and "b" is for ball, I decided to send her future self 26 dispatches from the concrete jungle she knows so well today, but that will be very different once she is grown. Night after night in the deep quiet of a house where a baby is finally sleeping, I set out to record for her, like some entirely unglamorous and Nutella-fueled Scheherazade, the stories that extended my brief stay in Costa Rica so far beyond its original date of execution: the reflections that, for me, go hand-in-hand with my favorite phrases and expressions.

I dedicate the following to the coffee field. To my daughter and husband. To the better angels of bus drivers. I dedicate it to Costa Rica, which bravely took me on as a college student, patiently tolerated my wandering twenties, and gave to me with open hands.

A NOTE ON COSTA RICAN SLANG

Every country in the world has its own sayings and expressions. I am biased, but I believe that Costa Rica's are among the most colorful, numerous, and hilarious. I also think it is safe to say that Costa Ricans are much more conscious of, and proud to share, their sayings than many other peoples in the world. It will probably be a source of lifelong frustration to me that when I use those sayings in conversation with people who don't know me well, I will always be met with surprised laughter. I said in a meeting recently that I was "*detrás del palo*" (behind the tree/branch, which in the United States we would translate as being out of the loop) and triggered a flurry of amused chuckles.

I have learned most of my favorite phrases from my husband and friends, although I am indebted to Carlos Arauz's *Dichos y refranes costarricenses: Frases y expresiones de nuestra habla popular* (2008), which I bought from the author at a book fair a few years back and found to be fascinating, as well as María Mayela Padilla's wonderful *Dichos y refranes de los ticos* (2013). Please see the Endnotes for more information on these works and others cited throughout the book.

Some of the phrases I present here are not specific to Costa Rica. Others are unique to this country, including words from Costa Rican *pachuco*, slang of a complexity I think is comparable to rhyming Cockney. Since Costa Rica is the only Spanish-speaking country in which I've ever lived, I do not always know the difference, so I apologize for the hodgepodge. I also offer my apologies for any misinterpretations or errors I might make as a non-native speaker presenting, explaining, and translating these expressions. After all, *aunque el mono se vista de seda, mono se queda*: a monkey dressed in silk is still a monkey, and a *gringa* a *gringa* no matter how many *chicharrones* she's eaten.

A lot, by the way.

March 26, 2004

Drinking fancy coffee under the vast Arizona sky that, for the past three years, has been tamped down firmly at the edges, enclosing my life. Not a block from where I sit on this café terrace after a run along dry canals and bridle paths are my car, my apartment, my two roommates. And yet the edges of my world, the enormous ring where that deep-blue sky meets the red desert earth, are starting to lift up now, to loosen, giving up their Tupperware grip. I can almost hear the "pop" and the rush of air coming in. I am restless.

Since my first stomach-turning day as a classroom teacher three years ago, I've collected a master's degree, beloved friends, a few tales of romantic misadventure, and countless mementos of pedagogical highlights and failures. But my thoughts have been turning to Costa Rica, and those two blissful months I spent there during college. I think I want to head back there, look for work, see what happens.

Not much of a life plan.

"Do it," my brother wrote to me yesterday. "Go now, while you can. Why not?"

As I sip my coffee I've been thinking of coffee beans, coffee plants in steep rows. On this terra-cotta plain, I can't stop picturing the lushness: mountains and mountains of it glimpsed from bus windows. All that green, extravagant, like money being spent. Like life about to begin.

ANTIGUO HIGUERÓN

LOST AND FOUND

Dear E,

Ten years ago today, I sat on an airplane listening to the "alright" chorus of "Float On" by Modest Mouse, and hoping it would be. All right, that is. In the belly of the plane just beginning to break through the clouds was a suitcase holding some clothes, two paperback books, and a few other sundries. The damp green valley coming into view below me held no reliable work prospects and only a temporary place to live through a former colleague. For once in my life, I had no idea what I was doing.

Only three years before, I'd watched bug-eyed from another plane window as I caught my first glimpse of the desert landscape of Phoenix, Arizona, home of my first grown-up job. There, in a place that looked to me like the surface of Mars, I found friends and carved out a place for myself amid the rocks. Now I had uprooted everything again for no clear reason, just to chase some happy memories from a college internship years before. I'd said I was going to work on my Spanish, but in fact I mostly hoped to tread water for a few months as I plotted my next move in life. As I sat there on the plane, it occurred to me that maybe I was a bit of a moron. It was one of my stranger ideas, this one-way ticket I'd bought to a place I really didn't know that well. I told myself: it's okay. I can buy another ticket just as easily. Tomorrow, even. I only have to stay a little while. I'll be here six months, tops.

Ten years later, here I am. And why? Is it because I haven't been able to find my way back to the airport? Well, no, but that's a fate that could easily be imagined, because one of the many things I didn't yet realize about the city I was rapidly approaching was that there were no street names or numbers. As most any casual tourist quickly learns, the country is full of paragraph-length addresses involving phrases like "200 meters south of such-and-such church," or "100 meters northwest of the place where don Quincho killed the one-legged chicken that one time."

I learned this a few days after my plane touched down, when I foolishly ventured into San José for a job interview armed only with a street name when what I needed was a Tico-style address. I got off the bus from the sleepy town where I was staying and, finding that no one could tell me how to get to the newspaper office I needed to find, took off at my usual brisk pace for my first of hundreds of walks across the city. I walked past strip clubs and adult theaters, addicts huddled on the sidewalk, and emerged, still lost, into the district where the Judicial Branch looms high in nondescript beige buildings.

I walked right past the building I was looking for, where I would one day be hired as a reporter. I walked past the hospital just next door where you, my daughter, would one day be born. For the first time, I trod the sidewalk I would cross thousands of time on my way to and from work, or to and from appointments at the fertility clinic—the sidewalk where I would take my last steps as a nonmother. I walked past the little hospital driveway where your father and I would one day load you into your car seat for the very first time.

It is strange, today, to imagine ever being lost in a neighborhood I would come to know so well, a single city block that would bring me to you in more ways than one.

On my second day in San José, I took a bus to try to find the boarding house where I'd end up living. I asked the driver to tell me when we reached the roundabout the landlady had told me to seek out, but he didn't. I stayed on until the depot and sheepishly found my way to another bus starting its route back down through the pouring rain. I was the only passenger; the driver struck up an uncomfortable conversation with me. At one point he asked to shake my hand and, when I warily extended it, planted disgusting kisses on my indignant wrist. My arm snapped back to me like Elastigirl's and I thought: Am I going to be raped on a public bus? What do I do? A reassuring *señora* got on at the next stop, a savior in a sweater set. I scampered back to sit near her, sure I'd escaped certain doom.

By that time I'd realized that I was lost, on many levels. I missed my friends. I missed my family. I missed my job and the life I had built. I had no sense of direction—but then again, that was precisely why I'd gotten on that plane in the first place. When in doubt, roll the dice. I'd hoped that taking a leap of faith would show me where I needed to go.

The house we live in now, your first home, can be found through various landmarks. One of them used to be the Super Sindy, which was our neighborhood grocery store and a spectacularly odd place. It had a gym above the produce section (creating an uncomfortable proximity between my lettuce leaves and thickset guys dripping with sweat and Plastigel), a video store above the cleaning products, and strange seasonal displays that once included a Santa Claus mannequin stuck into a tent and surrounded by empty beer cans to promote a summer camping-goods sale. One fine day, the Super Sindy was bought out by a national chain. Shortly afterwards, when I gave our address, the taxi driver corrected me: "el *antiguo* Super Sindy." I was elated. The old Super Sindy! I had arrived! I had stayed here long enough to see something become "*el antiguo*"!

The most famous "old" address in our neck of the woods is the *higuerón*, the fig tree. When I arrived in this part of town, it had recently been cut down, so everything was given in meters from the old fig tree—*el antiguo higuerón*. But then it grew back again, so we're back to "*del higuerón 150 al sur.*" The *higuerón* looms large in Costa Rican postal lore. I once set up interviews for a reporter doing a story on this very topic for the *Los Angeles Times*. The Correos de Costa Rica director told her that Costa Rica needs to transform its system, to modernize, to change with the times: "We have to stop thinking about the fig tree."

Stop thinking about the fig tree. He has a point, of course, and Costa Rica certainly deserves a working postal system, but one reason that changes are so tough to implement is that the old way is dearly beloved. The Super Sindy and the fig tree made me feel at home. To this day, when a taxi driver comments on my accent, I comfort myself by pulling out all the stops and giving him an old-school address, mentioning *sodas* and *pulperías* that were demolished long before I ever arrived here. It's a language, an insiders' code, and when you're an outsider, these things ease your homesickness in a unique way.

So, to paraphrase the musical *Rent*, how do I measure ten years? In cups of really good coffee, certainly. In a decade-long, slow, eventually delicious relaxing. In *aguaceros, dichos, trámites, presas*, and epiphanies. I have lived here long enough for that one suitcase to sprout, like one of those magic sponges, into a houseful of books and photos and a Barack Obama chia pet and tiny baby socks and Legos and half-chewed Minnie Mouse stickers.

Long enough to clear my head.

Long enough to fall in love, and out of love, and in again. I'm not talking about your father—that was a gradual but unidirectional fall, no backsies. I'm talking about the country. I adored its gorgeous surface, then discovered its seamy underbelly, then came to love it again in a way that's real, like a marriage. And it is a marriage. It is the conscious choice of another. It is a choice that, to survive, must go beyond the uninformed thrill, must take into account the potholes and bureaucracy and keep on keeping on. It is a choice whose rewards are incalculable and astonishing.

Long enough for Santa Claus to pass out in a tent and, presumably, recover (although if Christmas ever falls short of your expectations, I'm telling you it's because Santa Claus got drunk at the Super Sindy).

Long enough for a fig tree to be cut down, and to grow again.

Long enough for you to arrive. And that's the thing. If the girl on the plane could have seen you coming, way off in the distance, she would have forgiven herself her foolish one-way ticket, which is why every life needs one of those, including yours, someday. As the wheels touched down, she would have thought: Well, all right then. All right. All right.

July 21, 2004

I stepped out of the glass doors of Juan Santamaría International Airport just a few hours ago, and it all hit me: that humid air I'd forgotten, the shouts of dozens of taxi drivers, the uncertainty of the situation I've willingly chosen. I pulled my whole life behind me on wheels and navigated the sea of people.

I needed to get to the home of a woman I'd met during my internship at the newspaper La Nación *four years ago. The editors showed unwavering patience with a college student still learning to write in Spanish, introduced me to the kindest host family on the planet, and gave me the best summer of my life. When I started dreaming of Costa Rica once more, that was where I turned, and my old supervisor has offered to rent me a room at her family's home outside of San José while I get settled.*

Armed with her address, I allowed myself to be hustled into a cab. I suddenly felt more confident as I shut my door, blocking out the din of the crowd. I've got this, *I thought.* I know this country.

The taxi driver gave me an unreadable stare.

"Never close a taxi door that hard again," he said. "You slam a door in Costa Rica, most drivers will throw you right out on the sidewalk. We take care of our cars." He followed this up with an encouraging smile and put the car into gear.

And so it begins.

BRETEANDING

AN INCREDIBLE TRUE STORY OF PEACE AND WAR

Dear E,

Yours is a country of peace. It abolished its own army in 1948 and has, more or less, never looked back. The fact that some Costa Ricans don't regard that as particularly astonishing just makes it all the more remarkable: disarmament is a simple fact of life.

This is also a country of gibberish. At least, it seemed that way at first to a galumphing gringa with textbook Spanish, maneuvering her way through bars and parties, listening to conversations in which only a few words were intelligible. During one of my first outings ever in Costa Rica, as I sat dismayed and lost amid a group of Ticos, one of them turned to me and said, "I thought you spoke Spanish. Don't you?"

No. I didn't, not in the way he meant. I didn't, because Spanish, in the U.S. high school sense, was not the language being spoken around me, as my smirking interrogator knew full well. But at this particular gathering, I had neither the knowledge nor the energy to argue: I was not only at a linguistic disadvantage, but also recovering from the strain of my entrance. It had been my first experience walking into a social event where all four walls have a row of chairs pushed up against them, and all eyes turn to you, and you go from chair to chair, kissing their occupants on the cheek. For a New Englander, that's a marathon of intimacy. I was spent.

As time went on, I got used to all the kissing, but the language remained mysterious—no word more so than *tuanis*. It is a classic *costarriqueñismo*, or so I thought, meaning good, cool, great. Unlike many other slang words, however, it seemed to have no clear root. Where did it come from? What is its origin? People would tell me it came from Ticos trying to copy visiting gringos who kept saying "too nice," but that didn't ring true to me, mostly because "too nice" is not something we gringos tend to say.

As it turns out, the truth can't be found within Costa Rican borders. It lies to the north. *Tuanis*, as well as the more general Costa Rican tendency to switch the syllables of its words—*primo* becomes *mopri*, *fiesta* becomes *tafies*—has its roots in Nicaraguan *malespín*. This is a specific type of slang apparently based on a code created by Salvadoran General Francisco Malespín, whose military exploits took him around the region (including to Nicaragua, where he sacked León) and who also served as president of El Salvador in the 1840s. In his code, the syllables of words are rearranged and certain letters are switched around: *a* for *e*, *i* for *o*, *b* for *t*, *f* for *g*, *p* for *m*, and vice versa. Try this for the word *bueno*—*b* becomes *t*, *e* becomes *a*, *o* becomes *i*. What does that spell? Yup, *tuani*, which became *tuanis* during its southward migration to Costa Rica. It seems that this emblematic Tico word has a fascinating Central American tale to tell.

Here's another classic *malespín-ismo*. Take the word *trabajo* (work), exchange the *b* and *t*, and switch each *a* for an *e*, the *o* for an *i*. You get *breteji*, eventually shortened to *brete*, the slang for work that has become one of my favorite words over the past ten years. Its fascinating origins are only one of the great things about it. I love its Spanglish-tastic variant, *breteanding*, and there's something uniquely satisfying about *breteada*, a huge mountain of work, as in *"Vieras qué breteada me pegué anoche."* Just saying it makes you breathe out a little knot of tension: bre-te-AHHH-da. Most of all, however, I love the attitude adjustment the word *brete* has given me during my time in Costa Rica, because it's so often tied to the concept of gratitude.

"I'd love to stay, but I have so much to do. *Mucho brete. Gracias a Dios."*

"I was up all night working, and now I have a triple shift. I just taped my eyelids open and drank three quarts of coffee. *Mucho brete. Gracias a Dios."*

"My boss is the worst. I wouldn't mind feeding her limb by limb into a wood chipper. But hey, *tengo brete, gracias a Dios."*

In a Catholic country, this turn of phrase might be a reflex for many. It's sometimes more of a linguistic habit than a heartfelt sentiment. But as a foreigner and a person who almost never says "Thank God," it was jarring to me at first—then eye-opening. Over the years, it has become a powerful reality check. In any country, in any culture, those of us with the outrageous good fortune to find employment whenever we need it run the risk of forgetting what a privilege it is to put food on the table. Those of us who have only known the stress of over-employment forget how much more stressful it is to be under-employed. I don't say *gracias a Dios* in this context myself—it would feel affected—but the simple act of hearing it again and again has made me stop myself, at least sometimes, in the midst of a complaint or a rant. And it means that for me, *brete* is not just a word. It's a reminder.

It is late November as I write this. I am preparing for your second Thanksgiving, which will be my eleventh in the land of *tuanis*. I peel potatoes as you bumble around underfoot. I keep one eye on the stuffing while trying to keep you from ingesting your weight in Legos. I buy a chicken instead of a turkey, both because of the price and because a turkey won't fit in our tiny gas oven. I anticipate another feast that will feature a last-minute expat ingredient substitution no matter how much I plan. I put on some soccer as I cook and pretend it's the background noise of the football game I only crave one day each year.

As I do all that, I am grateful for you. I am grateful for the strangeness of a world where a general who destroyed a city also created a new way of speaking, and where a country that abolished its army has a centuries-old military code on its lips. Last but not least, I'm grateful for—well, I'd tell you, except I've gotta run, because *vieras qué montón de brete tengo que hacer hoy.*

Gracias a Dios.

July 30, 2004

Nine days since I returned to Costa Rica. Feels like nine years.

Was offered one job and took another. I moved from my former supervisor's lovely but somewhat isolated home to a rooming house just outside the heart of the city, on the edge of the University of Costa Rica campus. My roommates are a Costa Rican doctor, a Cuban historian getting her PhD, a friendly Australian wrapping up a journalism internship around the corner, and a group of Nicaraguan dental students. Mine: a small, narrow room that looks out over a concrete wall topped with rings of barbed wire, a similarly narrow bed that's not long enough for my feet, a bedside table, and a closet. I will pay for this by teaching English for $6 an hour—an unfavorable rate given that each hour of teaching requires more or less two hours on the bus.

I keep wondering what I was thinking. Even if I do make some friends and see a few new places, will it be worth all this? Tonight I went to see a movie in the gargantuan mall down the street; in the commercials before the previews, a dog pushed a TV across a living room so his owner would see an ad for flea and tick medicine. The entire theater broke out into gales of laughter and expressions of delight. I felt like an alien.

C AFETAL

A DISAPPEARING WORLD

Dear E,

Part of becoming a parent is gaining the ability to wax poetic about some pretty mundane shit—including, well, shit. Enough bleary-eyed diaper changes will make a philosopher out of anyone. Nothing, though, can compete with a bubble wand in terms of making a person ponder the fleeting nature of life. In the movie *Knocked Up*, Paul Rudd's character describes it: "I wish I liked anything as much as my kids like bubbles. . . . It's totally sad. Their smiling faces point out your inability to enjoy anything."

It's really true. Watching a kid chase bubbles puts us, as adults, to shame: the simplicity of the game, the intensity of the joy. I'm not sure I'd call myself unable to enjoy anything, but adults don't tend to shriek and jump up and down very often (something to shoot for). At the same time, kids playing with bubbles are a double-whammy reminder of the passage of time. Of mortality, even. I watched you in our garden yesterday, a little girl who is bigger and toothier and smarter every day, gleefully chasing generation after generation of tiny shimmering orbs that last only a moment. That's why they drive you wild, of course. A baby will grab a toy and tire of it quickly, but bubbles won't be grabbed. They can't be had. They burst on your fingers, leaving only a soapy slick. Every new bubble that floats out of the wand is a new challenge, an unattainable goal. A few seconds, and *murió la flor*, the expression round these parts for the end of something, for the moment when the fat lady has sung. I can't figure out where it came from—the flower has died— but it's not my favorite. I don't like endings, anyway.

I've mentioned the coffee field, or *cafetal*, in our neighborhood, the remnant of what was once an enormous plantation covering our entire sector of the city. Finca La Flor, it was called, according to a taxi driver who grew up among its plants and described it to me once on a ride. Our section is the last holdout. I always knew its days were numbered, given the real estate values around here; it doesn't even look that nice, since people tend to toss their trash at the edge of the fence, but I hoped and hoped that it would stay.

The other morning, as I rushed off to somewhere or other in a foul mood, I turned the corner and found that the section of the field closest to our house had been razed. *Perfect*, I thought. *Murió la flor. Murió Finca La Flor, y murió la flor.* I don't know for sure what's coming, or if the rest of the field will follow suit and give way to an enormous concrete housing development. I don't really want to know. But it's a change, and I don't like it.

"Will we still hear crickets at night?" I asked your dad later, like a little kid. I've always figured the proximity of the coffee field was the reason why our neighborhood at night is quiet and crickety in the way of New Hampshire summers.

"Yes," he said, grumpily. He hates crickets, which to me is like hating adorable bunny rabbits. "They're very happy in our garden." Then he looked thoughtful. "Really, it's a miracle that field has lasted all this time."

I guess it is. And I guess, as Pema Chödrön explains, "we are like children building a sand castle . . . we know that the tide will inevitably come in and sweep the sand castle away. The trick is to enjoy it fully but without clinging, and when the time comes, let it dissolve back into the sea." Man, but that's hard. I'm not good with detachment. I don't like things I love to be fleeting—certainly not people, and not coffee fields, and not even bubbles. Maybe that's what I'm supposed to learn from you: to be a glutton for punishment, to take maximum joy in things that can't last, to shriek every time bubbles emerge from the wand, to try and try again to catch them. To giggle, rather than frowning, when they disappear.

One evening when I was eight months pregnant, I felt like taking my belly for a walk, so you and I headed out into the dusk. I strolled to the corner and down toward the coffee field. There, on the jumbly porch of the caretaker's run-down wooden house, sat a handful of men, feet up on the porch rail, drinking *guaro* by candle-light. One played a guitar and a few more sang. A dog had collapsed at their feet. It was January, so the coffee cherries were at their ripest deep-red sheen against the sea of green plants that surrounded the house. Except for Homer Simpson on one man's shirt, the whole scene could have been 50 years ago, or 100.

I rested my hands on you, feeling no kicks: the short walk had lulled you to sleep. I stopped, suddenly unselfconscious, and gazed at the little tableau before me. The men on the porch saw me standing there, tall gringa and big belly, and waved so enthusiastically that their candles flickered in the gloom. A stubborn acre of coffee plants murmured in the summer wind. Our fragile bubble blew skyward.

July 31, 2004

Rain: quite a bit, more than I remember from my college intern days. Every day, sometimes all day. Tonight when I got home from teaching my afternoon class, I went into the kitchen to find two of my roommates studying, a younger guy I've never met painting a plaster model of the bottom teeth, and all three listening to my CD player, although how they could hear anything over the sound of the rain was beyond me. I brilliantly observed, "I think there's some water coming in"—then noticed the pots and plants strategically placed all over the kitchen to catch the leaks. Getting back to my own little cell, I found a column of water dripping down onto my nightstand.

So here we are: Nicaraguan dental students, a tooth-mold painter and I, catching leaks in a little San Pedro house, listening—I can now hear, since the rain has stopped—to disco classics. Where else would I be?

IAY, MAMI
LEARNING MY PLACE

Dear E,

When you're comfortable in a place, it's the little things that can remind you that you're not in Kansas anymore—like the volcanic ash that coated cars and roofs this month with a fuzzy layer of gray and forced motorcycle messengers to wear paper masks to protect their lungs, making the streets of San José look a little like Beijing. Usually, though, when a volcano isn't erupting, it's language that reminds me I'm still a foreigner: the words I still don't understand, or others that I do understand but that may never feel natural to use.

There are several words that fall into that latter category. One is the most famous Costa Rican phrase of all, "*pura vida*"—pure life, how's it going? no problem, we're cool, I'm fine, sounds good, thank you, you're welcome, see you later. I love this all-purpose expression, but usually avoid saying it because even after a decade, it still feels touristy on my lips. Another is the similarly all-purpose "*diay*," which can mean everything from "What can I tell you?" to "Where have you been?" It can be an expression of amazement or sheepishness or uncertainty when no other word will do, but it still doesn't sound natural coming out of me.

A third example is the common use of "*mami*" and "*papi*" as a way to address a very young child. "Come here, *papi*, let me tie your shoes." "No, no, *mamita*, don't touch that." I find it charming, but it is strange on my English-speaking tongue—it sounds like I'm addressing you as my mother, even though that's not the way it comes across in Spanish at all. Anyway, that is how I felt about it until yesterday, when I came around very suddenly.

You see, this month I added another job to the mix. I have been freelancing since you were six weeks old or so, with plenty of late-night slogs, full days and even international trips, so I thought that this new endeavor wouldn't change things too much—but I underestimated how different it would feel to have, for the first time in two years, a regular daily work schedule.

As soon as I sat down in my new office, I felt a sinking sensation totally at odds with the pleasant space around me and the kind people just outside my door. It was a knot in the gut that I instantly recognized from the day my parents dropped me off at sleepaway camp when I was 11 years old. It was homesickness. I thought about you back at our house and wondered what you were doing, just as I once lay in a bunk in Maine as darkness gathered above the lake outside and wondered what my parents were doing at home many miles away, yearning with my whole body to be back where I belonged.

I've been a little heartbroken, dealing with this transition, but I know it's part of the deal. There's a *dicho* for it, of course: "*Al que quiere celeste, que le cueste*," which literally means "if you want it blue, you'll have to work for it," but more roughly equates to "no pain, no gain." I believe that women and men are equal. I believe that women deserve equal access to education and an equal chance for professional success and, of course, equal pay for equal work. I believe that women should be able to marry in order to be loved, not in order to be supported financially. I believe all that, and I have had the great good fortune to be able to live like that. That's my gain. Now, here's the pain. Walking away from you as you stand at our garden gate is the pain. Missing a new gesture, a new word, a new discovery is the pain.

Just to be clear, when I say "no pain, no gain," I'm not referring to women who aren't given adequate maternity leave (hats off, USA), or aren't given the legal benefits they deserve. That's not equality; that's injustice. That's harmful to women, men and children alike, and is something we must address. No, I'm talking here about the inevitable pain that comes with the equally inevitable separation from the person we once carried within us, even when we've had time and space to adapt to motherhood, as I certainly have and as every mother should. Even when our rights and needs as parents have been respected, even when we're being separated from our kids at a reasonable age, for short periods and by the standard economic realities that affect most of us—it still sucks.

Yesterday, as I got ready to leave for work, I was suddenly overcome and sat down for a quick, efficient cry. You marched over, wearing the ruffled skirt and rubber rain boots you had picked out and put on all by yourself, and pulled your skinny body up onto my lap. What got me was the look on your face. You looked concerned, but not in a wobbly chinned, scared baby way. You looked concerned in the slightly amused but kindly way of a kindergarten teacher who knows the world isn't ending, but wants to find out why her young charge thinks it is.

Wearing that wise, benevolent expression, you took my face in your hands like a too-good-to-be-true child in a bad movie, one of those dimpled, cutesy kids who say unrealistic things like, "But mommy, all I want for Christmas is you." Only it was breathtaking instead of annoying, because you're not too good to be true. You poop all over the house and lick your Play-Doh as if it were ice cream and do all the other things real toddlers do. Still, here you were, hovering at my side like a good little fairy.

"What's wrong, *mamá*?" you asked. "Are you sad?"

"I'm a little sad," I said, "but I'm okay."

You considered this. "Is the baby sad?" This meant you.

"No, no! Everything is okay."

"Is Daddy sad?"

"No, he's happy, too! And I'm okay. I just love you, and I miss you when I go."

You tilted your head to one side and patted my head as if I were a friendly dog. "Don't worry, *mamá*," you said. "Don't worry."

All I could think was, *diay*.

I was otherwise wordless, astonished. You had never done anything like that before. I gave you a hug, pulled myself together, and headed out down the hill on the first leg of my walk to work. As my feet carried my reluctant body away from you, I saw your life flash before my eyes, your many faces: serene and big-cheeked in the ultrasound photo, scared and wide-eyed in a dark car seat during your first nighttime taxi ride, squishy and sleepy in your baby carrier. And now, pert and winsome and commanding and ringed by shaggy hair, as you look when you come to our room in the morning holding your parents' slippers. You hold them out to us and say, "Put on SHOES! Let's GO! One, two, three, four . . ." and you're out the door, waiting for us to follow.

I thought of all this, and realized what my reply should have been when you so expertly took charge and cajoled me out of the house. I sent the words back up the hill behind me, back to the garden where maybe, just maybe, you were still looking after me, although it was much more likely you had disappeared into the house like a shot looking for open drawers and Apple products. I sent a title you've earned already, one I have a sneaking suspicion you'll earn again and again in the years to come.

"Okay, *mami*," I said. "I won't worry, *mamita*. We're okay, *mami*, we're okay."

August 2, 2004

I walk a lot these days to get to the English classes I teach for customer service agents at industrial parks way across town. Every day I walk the pedestrian boulevard that spans the city center, past singing buskers and lottery-ticket sellers and a statue called "La Chola," a fat lady whose hand and rear have been caressed shiny-smooth by passersby.

It was been good training for last night: One of my Nicaraguan roommates asked me if I'd like to walk 13 miles along a highway in the dark with her and with some man she met recently somewhere, to see a statue of the Virgin that performs miracles. I said yes, of course, because that seems to be who I am at the moment. We set off on what I pictured as a strange, lonely walk, but turned out to be a stream of hundreds of thousands of people strolling, chatting, singing through the night until we reached the teeming square of the Basílica in Cartago. It was the annual pilgrimage to see "La Negrita," the Virgin of Los Angeles, Costa Rica's patron saint.

The pressure of the surging crowd lifted me off my feet and wafted me into the center aisle of the church, meaning that I was required to make the final leg of my journey on my knees. (Some members of the faithful make the entire trip that way.) This, I did not enjoy, and I was more than ready for some magical concoction called Cofal Fuerte that was thrust at us in little packets as we waited in line for a bus back home. "Put this all over your legs," my friend instructed, and I found that pepperminty bliss soon followed.

As we rode home, I thought about La Negrita, whose tiny form I'd barely glimpsed when my crackling knees finally made it to the front of the church. The people around me were thanking her for any number of miracles: sicknesses cured, disasters averted. I was too overwhelmed to thank her for anything except the journey's end.

STAR MEDIO 35

IF THIS IS INSANITY THEN CALL ME CRAZY

Dear E,

I've heard it a few times over the years, but now that I myself am 35 years old, one day it hit my ear in a new way. I had to ask your dad. "Why is it that '*medio treinticinco*' means crazy? Is that the age when you lose your mind?" *Uuy, pero ese mae está medio treinticinco, huevón.*

He explained that, no, there is a simple explanation: 35 is, or at least it was at some point, the police code for a nutcase. It's the number that crackles over the radio when a cop picks up a guy who thinks he's a chicken, or anyone with delusions of being able to cross San José in less than two hours during rush hour. Despite this clarification, however, I can't help but associate the expression with my age—which is my favorite age thus far. That's partly because of you, but also partly because blowing out candles 35 times seems to have freed up something in my brain. Or maybe it knocked something loose.

Sorting through mementos at your grandparents' house this summer, I spent more time than usual thinking about my childhood. A photo of a tanned, long-legged fourth grader brought back a memory: that year at school, for a while, the fad at recess was to run as fast as you could. It wasn't a PE drill or a game of tag. We'd just run helter-skelter until our hearts pounded and our throats ached. I can still see the distant fence coming closer across the field. It was pure joy.

In fifth grade—different teacher, school, city, and state—recess got more complicated, and it stayed that way for more than a decade. Being cool gets in the way, whether you are or you aren't. As my daughter, you already understand instinctively that I fall squarely into the latter category. (And if there were any doubt about that, the rest of the mementos I found this summer put that doubt FIRMLY to rest. To wit: the sixth-grade love interest who wrote me a yearbook message in Latin. Or the sixth-grade me who thought that was awesome.) In some ways, that makes life easier: I was smart enough to know a lost cause when I saw one in the mirror and to be fairly content with nerd-dom, at least some of the time. But most teenagers and plenty of adults waste energy, even tears, on fitting in, and I certainly wasted my share.

This year, I've found myself spending more and more time running as fast as I can for sheer pleasure, so to speak. I have told off more people than in the previous 34 years combined, and no longer mind so much if that annoys them. I have surprised myself by asking for what I am worth without any of the embarrassment I would once have felt. At the same time, I no longer listen to those who think that quiet, well-mannered, reticent people are inherently weaker or worse, because that's wrong, too. My definition of success has become broader. "No" has become much easier to say.

So has "yes." I joined a neighborhood aerobics class, which, and I say this with love, is about as uncool as you get. There's one girl who looks like Gisele Bündchen, but most of us look pretty goofy as we dance around—or sweaty, or dumpy, or totally lost. Suddenly, I don't seem to care. Maybe it's because there's a small person at home now who thinks all the silly things I do are hilarious, but looking ridiculous at the community center has somehow become a lot of fun.

I look at you, so tiny, and wish I could protect you from becoming self-conscious, but adolescence is a giant wall we all have to climb over to get to the freedom on the other side. What's more, if you don't deal with things in adolescence, you just have to deal with them later in life, as any orthodontist will tell you. That wasted energy and those wasted tears might not be wasted at all if they bring us closer to peace of mind.

Still, I'll be rooting for you to discover coolness nice and late, and shake it off as quickly as possible. Run as fast as you can for no reason whatsoever. Embrace your *treinticinco,* and cherish any birthday that helps you loosen up and dance.

September 9, 2004

I don't see my roommates too often in the evenings, so I have been leaving melodramatic notes on my bed when I go out in case I am abducted or murdered: "Went to Jazz Café 4 September 8 p.m." What good does that do? I don't know, but I write them out nonetheless. I have been looking for things I can go and see without being obviously alone or spending much money: shows, games.

Last night: Bar by the university for the Canada-Costa Rica game. It was packed, no seats, so I leaned against a pillar and sipped my Imperial, happy to feel that I was part of a crowd. As soon as my beer was empty, the waitress brought another. I told her I hadn't ordered it.

"He did," she said, gesturing toward a table in the corner where three guys sat watching the game. One looked over at me and made a little gesture that was part wave, part "come over here," his hand pointed down, one-two-three. (I've learned that Ticos don't beckon.) He glanced at the fourth chair at their table, empty, and smiled at me.

As the notes left on my bed imply, I am prone to worrying about worst-case scenarios, but something about him put me at ease—he had a kind face—and I was tired, so I went over and sat down.

His name is Adrián, and he is funny, sharp, and very critical. He was happy to learn I share his love for Joaquín Sabina, then terribly disappointed when he learned which of Sabina's songs is my favorite. It was nice to sit in a group for a change. Adrián said we should hang out again, maybe watch another game.

F

UTBOLÍSTICAMENTE HABLANDO

THE FEARLESS ONES

Dear E,

Our neighborhood is usually quiet on Sunday morning, but this past Sunday it was as solemn and still as a church. As I left you at home with your dad and trotted down the hill to start my run, I could hear the hushed voices of the altar guild: the barmen of our local watering hole, who behind their barricaded doors were cleaning glasses and righting overturned bottles after an insanely prosperous evening. I huffed and puffed up the hill beyond, past houses of Ticos dreaming of Jesus Christ—the Cristo de Río de Janeiro, that is, to whose photo someone added a Costa Rican soccer jersey in an image circulated widely on Facebook the night before. As I settled into the rest of my usual route, I realized that on this Father's Day, men all over the country were waking up, looking skyward, clasping their hands in prayer, and thanking God for the best gift they could possibly have imagined.

All of this was because on Saturday night, five million Costa Ricans had a religious experience. They watched their National Team defeat Uruguay 3-1 at the World Cup in Brazil. It is difficult to put into words how improbable, how miraculous, how terrific this victory was. "Passion of CHRIST!" said one fan next to me as we watched the game on TV at a party. "Son of a WHORE!" said the others, over and over, astonished beyond any other words as Costa Rica scored goal after goal against the two-time world champion. The suffix "-*azo*," roughly translated as big, giant, tremendous, is often slapped onto words to refer to a historic soccer victory that left a rival spinning, and this one is being called the *Uruguayazo*. It was one of the biggest days in Costa Rican history, *futbolísticamente hablando*.

Futbolísticamente hablando. In terms of soccer. Socceristically speaking. This is not national slang, of course, but simply one of my favorite phrases in the Spanish language. I was watching a post-game analysis with your father years ago when my ear first caught this phrase, tripping off the tongue of a slick-haired sportscaster. My jaw dropped.

"Did he just say '*futbolísticamente hablando*'?"

"Yes, of course," said your dad.

He couldn't understand why I thought it was so fantastic. I'm not sure I do, either; it's just such a specific and complicated term, one that captures the intense seriousness of soccer in Latin America and most of the rest of the world. It is also a combination of words I find bewitching and fun to say. If your dad hadn't stopped me, that might very well have been your name. "*Futbolísticamente-hablando*, you clean up your room RIGHT THIS MINUTE!" We can still change it, if you'd like us to.

You had a tough time during the *Uruguayazo*. Every time the room erupted in screams and shouts, you winced and gazed about in deep concern, running for my legs if you'd been walking around, or squeezing me tight if you'd been on my lap. I'd spring to my feet and bounce you gently, talking into your ear and trying to soothe you. Your chin wobbled in a pre-cry, known in Spanish as "making spoons"—I guess because the chin wobbles and curves inward, spoon-like—but you didn't wail. At the end of the game, you even applauded, but very slowly and with a look of despair, as if to say, "I'll try to play along, but my heart's not in it. I don't understand why everyone is behaving this way. I expected more of you people."

Futbolísticamente hablando, you are a little fearful, a little shy, a little uncertain. In every other way, you are fearless. You enter a room as if everything and every person in it was created for your inspection and enjoyment. You point and announce, grin and touch. You greet every person you come across like an old friend. You shimmy into food courts or restaurants with your hands in the air, yelling a general "TAA ta TAA!", eliciting squeals of delight from tables of ladies who lunch. And when you're really rolling, you'll turn around, throw someone a smile over your shoulder, and give that lucky person a little butt shake.

I love this. I also find it a little intimidating, because I wonder how to protect this happiness and certainty. So much of what parents are supposed to do is not to teach or change, but rather to preserve what is already there. We see the untroubled friendliness of babies and hope that our fearful hearts won't influence them too much, even as we want them to stay safe and sound. I don't recommend that you shake your butt at random strangers later in life, but I hope you hold onto the idea that while bad people do exist, a friendly soul and a good conversation can be found in unexpected places. You might not burble in wonderment at the sight of a magazine stand or coffee filter once you're an adult, but I hope you will retain your belief that you deserve to take pleasure in marvelous things, big and small. Your confidence is breathtaking. I wish I could promise that nothing will ever shake it.

I can't promise that, of course. You will learn, from life and surely from me, a number of caveats and limits and lessons that suck. For my part, I will worry and worry and worry some more. I will cross my fingers that you never develop a penchant for skydiving; if you do, I will one day be the one squeezing you as you reassure me that it will be all right. But I do promise you this: Even as I worry,

I will also try to remember the joyous, shimmying baby before me now. Even as I warn, I will do my best to protect the merry spirit of the toddler who treated every supermarket and shopping mall as her own personal runway. I will keep in mind that you once walked with the fearless ones, and that I have walked with them, too, for all of us have our moments of freedom and thoughtless bravery. Oftentimes, those are the moments that shape our lives the most.

The fearless ones know what it's like to do something—not every day, but sometimes in life—that makes no sense other than in their own minds. The fearless ones give up what they know, take the harder path, take the unexpected job. The fearless ones say yes even when yes is risky, or say no even when no is hard. The fearless ones love deeply and recklessly, even though that is terrifying. The fearless ones walk into a room as if they deserve to be there, even if they suspect they might not.

After all, that's what it takes to stride onto a field before tens of thousands of fans and let the roar of that crowd drown out the chorus of doubt in your head. To play as if you have nothing to lose. To run like the wind because you can. To believe that you deserve to win, and by believing, make it so.

September 19, 2014

I've fallen into a rhythm of sorts. Daily bus, walk, bus, walk, teach, repeat, reverse. Nightly trip to the pulpería *on the corner, where I buy cans of tuna, bags of spaghetti, bananas, squeaky Turrialba cheese. Daily columns for a travel website that pays me $5 per column, so I write as many as possible (yesterday I wrote about squeaky Turrialba cheese). Weekly trip to the internet café across the university to check email. Weekly call to my parents from the phone booth down the street. Weekly movie with my lanky, quiet Cuban roommate, who turns on the ancient TV in the common area like clockwork on Saturday afternoons to watch Cantinflas, Mexico's comic legend. When one day she explains that the joke is his meaningless long-windedness, I finally start to laugh along.*

On Saturday mornings, there's the farmer's market with Lourdes, my pilgrimage companion. She knocks on my door and we hike the 20 minutes or so to the Feria de Guadalupe, where I buy sugary coffee and we peruse the aisles—Lourdes matter-of-fact, I wide-eyed and lost. "Tome," she says one day, "try this," and thrusts a fruit at me. I'm so surprised that I drop it. It turns out to be a mamón chino, *a relative of the lychee, which I've never seen in its natural state: red, spiky, like a monster. She convinces me to try it. It's delicious. I think: Maybe my life here is like that. Maybe there will be something nice in the middle once I get through the spiky outside.*

Because despite these routines, it's lonely. It was all my idea, but that makes it lonelier. I miss my family and friends, and dream about my students in Phoenix. When I'm not writing, my fingers are itching to write, because I have so few people to talk to. I spend a lot of time just sitting in the dim kitchen, scribbling like this, feet propped up on the base of the table in case our resident rats run through. All through the Costa Rican rainy season, I eat mamón chino *all alone, splitting open their scary bodies, feasting on their sweet little hearts.*

GRANDE

WHAT I'LL TELL YOU ABOUT LA SELE, 2014

Dear E,

I don't know what it's like not to be big. I'm from the United States, a big country in every way—size, population, loudness, impact on the world for better and for worse. I'm also 5'10", a giant in Costa Rica, hulking and lurching my way through San José. Years ago, a man behind me in line for an ATM said to no one in particular, *"Jueeeeeeputa, qué gringa más grande."* Once, in an office photo, I was asked to bend down at the knees in the second row so I would fit in the shot. I have, not a bird's-eye, but a tops-of-other-people's-heads view of many rooms I enter.

On the other hand, it looks like you, my Tica daughter, might turn out to be teeny tiny. You are small for your age, and as you run around at top speed, saying "Hi!" and "¡Gracias!" to everyone, I'm often asked by confused strangers, "How *old* is that baby?" It's odd for me, the one who's always asked to get things off the high shelves, to think of having a petite daughter. You're small in another way, too: You are from a country roughly the size of West Virginia, a country without an army, a country known in part for its love of diminutives. Even though you're half gringa, you will always have been born in a little nation at the waist of the Americas, and that will always be a part of your worldview. (Thank goodness.)

"*Grande*" is one of the first words a Spanish student learns, but even a simple word like this has layers of meaning. It means big, of course, but also great. It means grown up: what do you want to be *cuando seas grande*, when you're big? It can also mean old, as a little white-haired lady once explained to me after she referred to herself as "*una señora bien grande*" and smiled at my evident confusion.

Many Costa Ricans, lost for words as *La Sele* left low expectations in the dust again and again during this World Cup, turned to one word: *grande*. *Grande* Keylor Navas, the impossibly valiant goalie. *Grande* Bryan, Joel, Yeltsin. *Grandes todos*, they say. *Grande La Sele. Grande mi país.* This Sele has shown us—Costa Ricans, and all of us—what it means for a little team from a little country to be big, to be great, to be grown up, to be fearless, to be prepared, to prove itself against all odds. It's been breathtaking. It's a lesson I want you, tiny one, to take to heart.

La Sele has also shown us how to be small again. Your father is *grande*, grown up, with all the cynicism that implies. He watches *La Sele* as any real sports fan watches his team: as if he were single-handedly paying their salaries out of his own pocket. Even as this World Cup unfolded, he was still quick to criticize or sigh heavily, all a part of his attempt to distract himself from the sheer anxiety of unexpected hope. But as the games went on, I watched him lose his ability to doubt. I watched him turn into a six-year-old boy before my eyes. He couldn't help it. He was gobsmacked by joy. Only sports can do this to a person—or at least, only sports can do this to an entire nation at once. Only sports can fill a country with childlike pleasure in this particular way. (After Costa Rica's elimination today, instead of crying or wallowing, people took to the streets with just as much pride as before to celebrate how far they had come. *La Sele* will not come home with the Cup, but they're the only team in the world that gets to come home to a country full of Costa Ricans.)

That's why I want you to remember your first World Cup. That's why I'll cut out clippings and carefully fold up newspaper covers, store the little flag you waved today as we walked around our neighborhood, save the scorecard on which your dad painstakingly noted the result of every game and proudly wrote "Costa Rica" in the quarterfinal bracket. That's why we'll tell you, like old-timers, about Bryan and Keylor and Pinto, who vanquished the Group of Death. They showed small people how to be big. They showed big people how to be small. They reminded everyone who was paying attention that anything can happen, that a soccer field is a blank canvas, that little can be mighty, that old can be young, that it's always worthwhile to believe. That life is beautiful.

Tonight, on the first of the two buses I take home from teaching at the dental technology call center (between my roommates and my job, I have learned more about dentistry in the past two months than I ever hoped to), a man stood up and spoke for a long time. Glory to God, and so forth. Raise your hand if you believe in Jesus. He harangued tired people on their way home from what was probably a day spent on swelling feet, or a day of boredom behind a cash register, or just a day. He handed out yellow business cards advertising an evangelical radio station, and when one man wouldn't put his hand out to take it, the preacher said, "What? Christ asks to come into your life, and you say no?" The rest of us put out our hands meekly, there in our darkening seats.

Suddenly, I found that he had taken the empty seat beside me. He gestured toward the window I was contemplating. "What a beautiful panorama, no?"

I looked out at a massive dairy truck, a herd of fuming cars, a dark brown slab of dirt where an excavator stood like a drooping crane. "Yes," I said.

"So you speak Spanish? ¡GRACIAS A DIOS!" Hands flung skyward. "And where are you from?"

"Arizona."

"¡GRACIAS A DIOS! ¡Que Dios nos bendiga! Where they film the movies! I love watching a good Western. When I'm not in church."

Traffic choked along.

"I tell my wife—I tell her, if I hadn't been a minister, I would have been a pistolero in a Western de spaghetti." He laughed. "A pistolero! ¡Gloria a Dios!"

We rode on into the heart of the city, the priest's daughter and the minister who wanted to be a cowboy. Before our eyes, visions of dust, of the desert big and flat and hot.

ABLANDO PAJA

WORDS TO LIVE BY

Dear E,

Baby papá agua gracias.
Woo-woo uh-oh hot wow tick-tock pat up hi ok shoes ¡gooooool!
Quack daddy moo cat cold dog socks eyes shh!
Happy.

No, that's not a drunken New Year's Eve haiku. Those were your first 25 words, faithfully recorded by yours truly in the back of the little black-and-gold notebook I kept on you this year. They are on my mind tonight as you watch Mickey Mouse, I drink my beloved afternoon coffee, and the last traces of sunlight die away on this last day of 2014, a year to which I hate to bid farewell. After all, this was the year in which you learned to walk, run, and wear a full, upside-down bowl of cheesy spaghetti as a hat. Most of all, it was the year you learned to talk.

"*Hablando paja*" means talkin' straw, but is closest in meaning to "shooting the breeze." It can describe someone who is full of hot air or even lying, but to me it connotes only good things. In fact, of all the phrases in this book, this one might mean the most to me. In many ways, it is the cornerstone of our marriage: when someone has had a stressful day (usually me), or life is simply hard, the answer is always the same. Your father says, "*Vamos a la cama a hablar paja.*" When that time comes, I know it means there is nothing particular to discuss, that the conversation will meander, that there will be comfortable silences and little stories and my heart rate will slow to what I think of as its proper Costa Rican level.

This was the year you learned how to talk, but you have not yet learned to *hablar paja*. Everything you say is urgent and deeply important. "Come on, let's go!" you'll say with your purse over your shoulder (and by "your purse" I mean my purse, or an old bag of Goldfish crackers, or a wooden coat hanger, or whatever else you have decided is the accessory of the moment). "Look, the MOON!" you said to me just now on the way home from the supermarket, even though you had pointed out the moon two minutes before. "The baby is SAD!" you said throughout the day yesterday after we watched a *Henry Hugglemonster* episode that featured a momentarily sad baby monster; you repeated it with so much empathy and despair that it seemed the baby was all alone somewhere, waiting for you to come and solve its problems.

Someday, I trust, you and I will shoot the breeze. If we are lucky, we will exchange so many words that we will remember only a small fraction of them, and we will talk aimlessly while looking at skies and trees and maybe an ocean or two. So far, however, there is no *hablando paja* with you, which is how first words should be. Only after years of practice will the incredible skill to put into words what you are thinking or feeling become commonplace. For now, you recognize it as the superpower it actually is. You are still fresh from the silence inside my belly and then the screaming muteness of babydom. Nabokov wrote, "The cradle rocks above an abyss, and common sense tells us that our existence is but a brief crack of light between two eternities of darkness." That's why first words fascinate us so. They are a message from the void.

As I write, this quiet house is vibrant with promise. Your lips, still for once as you lie sleeping in your crib, hold the thousands of future words you will whisper, sing, and shout from mountaintops. The air coming through the open windows holds the faint scent of explosives, a promise of the fireworks that will rain down on our neighborhood in just a couple of hours to celebrate the New Year. Our fridge holds a big bottle of Imperial because, as the advertising slogan goes, *hoy es de litro*. It's a beer-by-the-liter kind of night.

It's a moment that's full of things to come, but it's also an ending, and it makes me think of last words. We don't get to choose them, of course. I do entertain a few hopes about mine, mostly that they're not "This footbridge seems a little wobbly," or "AAAAAH!" or "Shark!" I also hope they are spoken in extreme old age, in a hammock at the beach or a wooden Adirondack chair in Maine.

But I don't aspire to a particularly eloquent or lofty closing. I hope my last words are *pura paja*. "Do you think I should have another mojito?" would be ideal. "That cloud looks kind of like Danny DeVito" would be just fine, too. As I write this, the last words I have spoken were "Goodnight moon, goodnight air, goodnight noises everywhere," and while I certainly hope those weren't my last words ever, they'd do quite nicely.

At the same time, it'd be nice if my last 25 words, or at least my last thousand, had at least a little of the urgency and wonder of your first 25. Ideally, they will contain something worthy of this brief crack of light I love so much, this escape from the abyss, this cradle of life. I hope "happy," your lucky number 25, is among them. And "thanks." And "love." And "peace." And you, your name, many times over, because your name means all of the above.

September 24, 2004

Ever since I returned to Costa Rica and La Nación *informed me they were—unsurprisingly—in no condition to hire a non-native speaker of Spanish as a full-time writer, I have been dropping off my resume at* The Tico Times, *the English-language newspaper, to see if I can get some freelance work. No response of any kind, and then I get a call: would I be interested in a full-time position? Their business reporter is leaving.*

Long story short, I've got it. I start tomorrow. My Aussie roommate, who is heading home soon, brought me a beer earlier to celebrate. He reassured me when I pointed out I have no idea what I'm doing, really. Says I'll figure it out as I go.

When I think about my new workmates and new profession waiting for me tomorrow, I feel like a kid before the first day of school.

"They won't know what hit 'em," says my friend. "It's the dawn of an era. They'll call you Scoop."

ISLA

**WHAT I WOULD WHISPER IN
THE EAR OF MY NEW-MOM SELF**

Dear E,

"Isla" is the name of the baby a friend of ours is waiting to bring into the world at any moment, just across the city. I have been thinking a lot about this lovely word, Spanish for "island," and have concluded that it's the perfect name for a baby because birth sets us adrift. She comes and lifts anchor and the family's off to sea, just the parents and that baby in one little boat. Even among partners, within your family, there are times when you're all in your own vessels, sailing close but separately, a wobbly fleet of love.

That is why no one can quite understand new mothers in those early days or weeks. If you ever become a mother, my dear, you'll find that any and all advice you receive (and there is a lot of it) is barely intelligible, as if it were being shouted across some vast space from a distant, unimaginable world. It is. It's coming to you across the water. It can be comforting or even useful, but the fact remains that no one knows what's going on in your own boat but you and the captain.

The captain is not you, by the way. Your baby has a plan for you, and you are along for the ride. In my view of things, parenthood doesn't start with birth. Not all of it, at least. It phases in, like childproofing. Many, many months into the journey, your child will do or say something that requires a stern retort, and you will come to as if out of a fog, and think, "Oh, shit! It's starting!" But that's later. For now, just ride. You are there to comfort and sing and feel your way in the dark and bail out the ship when it fills with the myriad fluids of newborn babydom, but you are not calling the shots. Not yet.

Let the waves come, murmur a seafaring song, and know this: in any moment of new motherhood that is rough going for you, there are countless like you. There are also others for whom that very same moment was transcendent and amazing, and you'll probably hear all about it. By the same token, in every moment that is wonderful for you, there are other women for whom that very same moment was terrible. Every ship takes its own course. Birth itself? As many experiences as there are women. First attempts at breastfeeding? Can be blissful, can be hellish, but no matter what, you're not alone. Even the first time you hold your baby can be euphoric, or wrenching, or terrifying, or all three, or something else altogether. It's all okay. Your boat will bob forward. Your baby may look feeble, but she knows what to do.

You won't be in your little boat forever. Soon you'll realize you've circled up with others, comfortably at anchor, jostling against each other quite companionably off the shores of that nonsensical, psychedelic land of toddlerhood. You'll notice all the boats now look a lot alike. Whether they were handcrafted from locally sourced unfinished wood with organic dyes or mass-produced using Chinese plastic, they're all covered in some sort of breakfast cereal and they all have a weird smell coming from *some*where. The mothers are the captains now, though mutinies are an hourly occurrence. These women have a lot more in common, at least within their groups, defined mostly by the presence or lack of a sense of humor. They share and support each other. They are becoming landlubbers.

And they remember you, out at sea, holding on for dear life. They remember you wistfully, even longingly, depending on the woman: you and your baby, alone on the waters, curled up in a rainstorm, mystified and awestruck, nursing each other into a brand-new world. They see your boat out there and remember their own, that place no one else could fully see, that place no one else could truly know, that place they will never, ever forget. They cup their hands and call out to you across the booming surf, annoying things like "Enjoy every moment!" or unhelpful things like "It goes so fast!" or essential wisdom like "Nipple cream! Nipple CREEEEAM!" And you bail out your boat and shake your head.

For your baby is already charting her course, this one-woman island, this launcher of fleets, the only one with the power to make you brave this particular ocean.

As for you, you will find your sea legs the only way they are ever found: amid the waves.

October 20, 2004

No time to write but will try anyway. I'm figuring it out, have a little notebook and pen and what else do you need? Struggled through my first interviews. Still asking secretaries and press people to repeat the phone numbers they rattle off so quickly all day long. Finding my way around the Legislative Assembly, the Judicial Branch, the personalities in our jumbly newsroom—including Snuffy, a mutt with an underbite who sleeps next to the publisher's desk and occasionally snaps at black dress shoes. Lots of gallo pinto *breakfasts, quick lunches, takeout dinners at our computers, late-night beers, especially on Thursdays, the night the weekly paper gets put to bed.*

> *Massive corruption scandals everywhere, complicated networks of alleged kickbacks that make me dizzy to think about. On my third day on the job, I got thrown out of a swanky private school where the wife of one of the major players is a teacher. My boss sent me to get a comment from her, surely knowing this would not end well. For some reason, maybe nostalgia induced by the seasonal bulletin boards in the hallway, I said to the guard as he hauled me out, "But I'm a teacher myself!" Then I remembered, that's not true anymore.*

JUNTOS PERO NO REVUELTOS

TRAVELING WHILE PARENTING

Dear E,

Every time I get to New York City, the first thing I want to do, right after I set down my suitcase, is run. It seems like the only appropriate response to a place with so much gorgeous ground to cover, so much energy steaming up through the grates. Twenty minutes after I got off the subway this time around, I was huffing and puffing my way through Central Park in the fresh, sunny sweetness of a spring I hadn't earned, happy as a clam. The words bouncing through my head like a mantra as my feet slapped Stateside sidewalks were "*juntos pero no revueltos. Juntos pero no revueltos.*"

Juntos pero no revueltos is an egg-inspired expression: together, but not scrambled. Together, but still independent. It's used to describe that need for breathing room and independence in a romantic relationship, friendship, or most any situation. It's been on my mind because I've been dreading this trip, only my third of any kind away from you, and the longest. I've been dreading our un-scrambling, however temporary.

Because you know what? I'm just a scrambled-eggs kind of girl. It surprised me to learn this when your father first moved in. I'd always thought of myself as a bit of a loner, and I expected to need lots of space. Who knew that I could be so content in another's company? Who knew that when it came to him, and now you, I would be such a *zorro de leña*, a fox in a woodpile, a homebody? (Since this might sound like one of those motherly boasts I so despise, I should mention that this doesn't make me a better wife or mother by any means—arguably the opposite, especially when I one day drop you off at school and bawl in the doorway. It's just a way of being, and one that surprised me.)

So I dreaded five whole days apart, and then, of course, I had a great time in New York. I walked walks and viewed views and ate the best chocolate cake on Earth. I wandered the aisles of The Strand and slept like a log. I realized how much I miss my country and this extraordinary city that has called my name since I was 20. I unscrambled.

This morning I went for one last run in Riverside Park. I wanted to stay forever. I wanted to move our family here. At the same time, I felt the pull of you and of our existing life, as clearly as if you were yanking on the world map from down below, wrinkling the surface of the Earth through sheer toddler insistence, bending the globe so that my sneakers lost their traction and I began to slide.

I stopped at the 91st Street Garden, basking in beauty, and I realized something I hope I won't forget. Maybe it was the rhythm of the cars on the Parkway, maybe it was the rattling of the subway underfoot, maybe it was my own clumsy breathing. Whatever it was, it made me see that while we might have personal comfort zones, we don't really choose between scrambled or apart. It's a heartbeat. One follows the other, over and over. You hug me, tight against my belly, where you first belonged, and the next moment you're wriggling to the floor like a desperate fish, shouting "How we gonna Play Doh *right now*?" And the heartbeat sounds, together/ apart. BoomBOOM.

You snuggle into my neck, like when you were tiny, and then arch your back to tell me it's time to put you down to sleep all by your lonesome. BoomBOOM.

I drop off the edge of our little world into a city you'd find as strange and wonderful as Oz, and then you pull me back again just as quickly, like a yo-yo; the trip seemed eternal at the start, but I know that the moment I lay eyes on you tonight, it will seem like the work of a moment. The blink of an eye. A vision. A dream. Boom-BOOM. BoomBOOM. BoomBOOM.

We are scrambled together; we are apart. It's not so much a balance as an acceptance that both will come, and go, and come again.

I breathed in the scent of the flowers one more time, wondering what you were thinking at that very moment, what you were touching—you who used to touch only me, you who were a part of me, just like my thudding heart. *Revueltos. No revueltos. Revueltos. No revueltos. Revueltos. No revueltos.*

That same rhythm drove me forward, and I ran on. I ran south, toward you, toward home. Toward the mists the sun was burning off the Hudson.

December 10, 2004

I had one of those moments this morning when all of a sudden, everything is worth it. I took the 6:00 a.m. bus to Puerto Viejo, on the Caribbean coast, to write a story on a soup kitchen that has opened up here for indigenous children. I got off the bus in the midmorning heat, and after asking around a little bit I started walking along a dirt road toward the kitchen.

I had a change of clothes on my back, my ratty reporter's notepad in my pocket, and all of a sudden I started grinning like an idiot. This was not only because I finally went on an official date with Adrián last night. It was all of it. It was because I could hear the ocean crashing to my right, and there was a cold beer and hot pati in my future, and I was here to learn about something interesting, and write about it, and get paid for that. Perfection.

ÁTERIN ES STALIN

THE IMMIGRANT'S SECRET IDENTITY

Dear E,

One day, not too long after you learned your dad's first name, you pointed to me and said, "Káterin!"

Your father laughed at my look of horror. He understood immediately that while "Káterin" is what he calls me, what everyone here calls me, I want my daughter, my own flesh and blood, to say my name the way my family does. With the people who share my genes, I want to be Katherine Stanley, not Catering Stalin, the label that awaited me on my clean clothes each week, back during my early years in San José when I took my laundry to a *lavandería*. Sometimes I want my *th* back, and our last name without an *eh* in front of the "s." Sometimes I want to hear my name the way I hear it in my own head.

But only sometimes. In general, I have come to love these little flourishes. It's all part of the immigrant secret identity. We take on different pronunciations, sometimes even different names altogether, and we blend in as much as we can, even though we'll always stand out. I have already told you how lost I was when I first came here. That's something I, like most immigrants, like most people of any kind, try to forget. With the exception of U.S. politicians who boast about their humble beginnings to the point of absurdity, we try to leave behind our lesser, unsure selves. There's a *dicho* for this, of course: *Ningún cura recuerda cuando fue sacristán.* No priest remembers being a sacristan. I looked up that last word, years back, and found that a sacristan is a church official—but since I didn't grow up with that title, I've always imagined that the priest forgets what it was like to be an altar boy (one of my favorite words in Spanish—*monaguillo*).

That's why immigrants—or expatriates, although the distinction between the two terms is a strange, classist and sometimes downright racist affair—sometimes withdraw from more recent arrivals. We don't want to be reminded of our own past selves, fumbling and vulnerable. We want to stay protected by the acquired knowledge that makes us feel at home and in control, even when we are not. When other people from our countries turn up unexpectedly in our neighborhoods, those other immigrants are blowing our cover, interfering with our vision of ourselves as unique and exotic. We're the odd one out, but we like it that way. Have at us, psychotherapists.

I now know these streets far better than any of my childhood roads. Your grandmother and her sister used to scrunch down in the back of their parents' car on the way home from the market in New Hampshire, closing their eyes and trying to figure out where they were on the familiar journey from Concord to Dunbarton, feeling every curve and turn. I can do the same now, but in a faraway city that would have seemed very strange and noisy to those young

New Hampshire girls, or to an earlier version of me. I suppose this makes me proud.

It's the same with motherhood, of course. They tell you, "They grow up too fast"—and we mothers forget just fast enough. We forget how clueless and scared and vulnerable we were. We forget why it was so complicated. I heard recently about a baby who cried all day and night and said to your dad, "We're so lucky our daughter never did that!" and he looked at me, shocked by my amnesia. I know that there was one day when I didn't have time to eat anything or pee from five o'clock in the morning, when you awoke, until two in the afternoon, when your dad got home from his shift. Why? What was I so busy doing? I can't remember, for the life of me. I am on firmer ground now, as a parent and a foreigner.

And yet. One night, six months pregnant with you, I rode my usual bus home late from work, texting with a colleague. I didn't notice that I'd missed my stop. The bus rumbled on to the end of its route. I had no idea where I was and am embarrassed to say that I even called your father in a momentary panic as I walked the dark streets in bemusement. I soon came out onto the main road and saw I'd been less than 20 feet from my usual running circuit, 50 from our supermarket. That is the fate of the foreigner: no matter how long we stay, how fluent we become, how assiduously we memorize local shortcuts and shorthand, we are only one block, one stop, one unfamiliar slang word away from being lost once more. This is the fate of the parent, as well: when we get too confident, our child will change, throwing us off balance or scaring the pants off of us all over again.

Sandra Cisneros said it best: "*When you're eleven, you're also ten, and nine, and eight, and seven . . . You feel like you're still ten. And you are—underneath the year that makes you eleven.*" Our previous selves are still inside us, nested like Russian dolls. I find this very comforting. It means that when you, my girl, are big and too cool for me, I can at least believe that the nutty toddler I know now, and the sweet, determined baby who came before that, will still be in there somewhere. Within the priest is the sacristan or the altar boy, awkward, new. Within the not-lost gringa is the lost gringa.

Within the confident mother is the terrified mother. Our old selves are just below the surface, and all it takes is a nudge, a glance, a taste, a sudden memory, a missed bus stop, to rearrange us.

This is usually humbling. With a little luck and grace, it does not have to be shattering. Life is easier if we can learn to smile upon the ten- and twenty- and thirty-year-olds who pop up to the surface unbidden. We do well to remember our nesting dolls, our forgotten altar boys, and extend a hand to them as old friends.

Katherine Stanley Obando   65

January 20, 2005

Met Adrián for a birthday breakfast, then went to a shelter on the west side of San José for my series on homelessness. Got a little lost, of course, but finally found myself in a room full of men, teenagers, and a woman scooping rice and beans onto plastic plates. I met a 14-year-old who was drawing at one of the emptier tables as if he were at elementary school. His drawing was labeled "Nicaragua, tierra de volcanes," and featured a big volcano, smoking black. He had come to Costa Rica to look for his older brother, who had come here to look for work, and things went wrong.

Another man, much older, was fashioning scorpions out of wire. His fingers were blackened and shiny. When he found out it was my birthday, he gave one to me, and a group of men sang.

They didn't know my name, of course, so they sang, "Cumpleaños feliz / te deseamos a ti / Cumpleaños, periodista." Happy birthday, reporter. I sat there in the big hall, basking in their kindness and in my job title. I took the scorpion back to the office and set it on my desk, right in front of the monitor, to remind me.

I am moving next month, away from this funny boarding house and posse of rats, up the hill. One of my roommates will be a fellow Tico Times *reporter, and the others all live within a five-block radius. It's near a supermarket with a weird name, a bus stop and a cafetal.*

LEÓN DEL BOLIVAR

ON MOTHERHOOD AND HUNGER

Dear E,

I've come to Costa Rica three times in my life. The first time, I was seven, on vacation with my dad, and I remember absolutely nothing about the whole trip except seeing an enormous crocodile in the canals of Tortuguero. The third time, I was 25, beginning the six-month visit that has continued for more than a decade. But in between was the college summer when I worked as a highly improbable intern at *La Nación*. As I mentioned before, the generous staff of this national newspaper allowed an eager college student to roam their newsroom and get her name in print. They also set up a homestay with the greatest family in Costa Rica.

Don Memo and doña Hannia sealed my fate, planting the seeds for my return years later. They ensnared me in a net of good food, exuberant kindness, and *costarriqueñismos* that I would never quite escape. In a very real sense, they paved my way to you.

Don Memo, the jovial patriarch, treated his gringo boarders like amusing pets, with excellent consequences for my Spanish skills. Whenever relatives came over, he'd make me stand in the middle of the living room and sing the national anthem, never dreaming I'd be grateful to him when I reported on, and then worked for, a series of Costa Rican presidents and had to sing the anthem at countless events. He'd also ask me to pronounce *otorrinolaringología*—the medical specialty we know as ear, nose, and throat—and chuckle over my missteps. And along the way, he introduced me to my first *dichos*, some of them wildly inappropriate. On at least one occasion, the stalwart doña Hannia overheard his instructions and said something along the lines of "Holiest Mother Mary! Katherine, don't you dare repeat that under any circumstances!" (Come to think of it, I could imagine a similar scene going on between your father and me, should we ever take in a completely naïve college student who mimics him like a parrot. Or, say, a toddler who repeats everything he says. Oof. I may be in trouble here.)

A tamer set of expressions, and very useful in that house, were the uniquely Costa Rican phrases to describe hunger and satiety. When you're starving, you're *como el león del Bolívar*, the lion at San José's Simón Bolívar Zoo. When you're full, you're *como la perrita del cura*, like the priest's little dog. Why? Well, because the priest had a little dog and always gave her plenty of table scraps. That's why. Which priest? Don't ask so many questions.

At Memo and Hannia's, I put away enough food to rival any lion. Every single morning, I'd stumble out of the little granny flat where I stayed up late reading Borges and Neruda, and meet the other boarders in the kitchen for a full Costa Rican breakfast: *gallo pinto* and eggs however we wanted them and fresh juice and fruit. Every evening, after a workday that invariably included both morning and afternoon coffee breaks with sweet pastries, and lunch in the cafeteria, we'd put away vast dinners followed by hot *arroz con leche* from the restaurant where their daughter, Alejandra, worked at the time. Then we'd pile into Memo and Hannia's bed with the entire family, or at least all the women, to watch that night's episode of *Mujeres Engañadas*, the telenovela that took my Spanish to a new level and taught me to say, *"Nunca, NUNCA te perdonaré"* with appropriate panache.

In short: we ate a ton. That was the summer I began running in earnest, just to combat those meals. Of course, I never knew I'd cover so many more miles of Costa Rican road a few years down the line. I left their house in tears one early morning in August of the year 2000, thinking I would never be back.

Sometimes I miss the hunger of those days, both literal and figurative. Every new food, I had to try. Every family gathering was fascinating. Every Friday night, we gringos would go out on the town, then rise at the crack of Saturday dawn—a few times, we stayed up straight through and grabbed a Ticoburguesa with greasy fries to tide us over—to hop on a bus to anywhere. I walked beaches in a state of bliss, stayed up all night dancing or talking about literature, drank my first and my tenth and probably my hundredth Imperial, listened to Sabina and Shakira for the first time ever, slept in a hammock at a jungle lodge near Puerto Viejo that I've never been able to find since. I was *como el león del Bolívar*, in every sense.

In this phase of my life, I'm the priest's little dog. It's Saturday night, quiet and dark. You're asleep in the next room. I can't go anywhere, and I don't want to. I'm comfortable here, full beyond my wildest dreams, as if the priest had put a full steak dinner under the table for me to feast on. This doesn't bother me in and of itself, except that it makes me wonder if I'm a failure of feminism, a career woman who has lost some part of her personality. What happened to that girl who wrote letters to every newspaper in Latin America until she got that summer internship? The girl who once told her favorite author she'd cut off her left arm to work for him (just the left, though—let's not exaggerate), prompting snickers at a Harvard auditorium but eventually landing the job? The girl who dreamed of diving suicidally into the worst school she could possibly find in New York City and starting a one-woman educational revolution? What happened, for that matter, to the girl who came back to San José on a whim and a prayer? The drive I used to feel is only a memory. I know I should say that now that you've come along, I feel more motivated than ever to change the world, but the truth is that at the moment the only motivation I feel is to spend as much time with you as possible.

Of course, part of growing up is that I don't want to sell myself short anymore. I have put in plenty of work since you were born, as a mother and a professional, and accomplished some amazing things. The difference is not so much in the result as in the approach. I no longer pursue work the way I once did. When I push myself, it seems to happen out of force of habit, as if I'm on autopilot after so many years of overachievement. The ambitious part of me seems to be dormant, albeit contentedly so.

There's no simple answer, but I find myself turning back to *el león del Bolívar y la perrita del cura*. I think that, at the risk of sounding overly biblical, there are times to be hungry, and times to be full. There are times to gulp down life one enormous steak after another, and times to loll under the table full of gratitude. There is room for a lion and a lapdog in all of us. I think that the ambitious girl I remember is still in here somewhere. Someday, surely, she'll find a new reason to roar.

June 11, 2005

Surreal few days. I got an interview with the Costa Rican ex-president who, after leaving office, became the first Central American ever to be elected secretary-general of the Organization of American States. During that term, he came back to Costa Rica to defend himself against allegations of corruption and was taken off the plane in handcuffs. He spent some time in preventive detention in one of the country's toughest prisons, albeit in an isolated section. His neighbor in the next cell was another former president also accused of corruption.

Today he is under house arrest, and gave The Tico Times *an appointment. I sat with him at a shiny table in his book-lined study in suburban Escazú. He gave my photographer colleague some tips about how to deal with back pain from carrying heavy equipment. He said he has discovered, for the first time, in total humiliation, the importance of love.*

I kept thinking of our first meeting, one he of course did not remember and that I did not bring up. I'd shaken his hand five years before when a political reporter at La Nación *let me tag along for the day as part of my internship. The president had just finished inaugurating something or other when we were introduced. I remember that he exuded confidence, a person at the top of his game, with great things behind and before him. He asked where I was from and when I said Maine, he replied, "The best lobster in the world!" This seemed hilarious for some reason, or maybe it was just that the day, the country, the moment seemed so perfect. We laughed and laughed.*

MACGYVER

THE TRUE SECRET OF HAPPINESS

Dear E,

Years before you were born, I was sitting at the rough cement table in our little garden with some friends. One was my former room-mate here in this house, who now lives in the United States but was back for a visit. She posed an interesting question over our beers: What is it, exactly, that makes life in Costa Rica so much more re-laxed than life back home?

"When I lived here, I wasn't lying on the beach all day," she pointed out. "I had a demanding job and worked long hours, just as I do now in the States. My relative income was fairly similar, as were my social and family obligations. This city is noisier and more crowded that my city back home. What is it, then? What is it about Costa Rica that makes life calmer?"

I thought about this for a long time. I think of it again every time a new study comes out saying that Costa Rica is the happiest country on earth, or the second happiest, or 93.2% happy, or what have you—an honor that many people I know receive with a certain bemusement as they battle traffic, or wait in long lines, or pick their way through oceans of litter on a morning walk. Like my friend, I, too, have worked like a donkey (as you'd say in Spanish) for most of my years in this country, logging my share of 14-hour days under fluorescent lights. As a reporter, and then working in government, I have seen aspects of Costa Rica that are unflattering, exasperating, and downright infuriating. But there is an underlying cheerfulness among the people here that seems to survive most any setback or annoyance, an unruffled approach to life that does seem rather mysterious, and that I think has gradually worked its way into my bones over the years. What's in the water?

I have finally come to a conclusion that is completely anticlimactic, like most of life's secrets. I believe that Costa Ricans, or many of them anyway, have a more peaceful life simply because they prioritize that. They put a higher premium on well-being and tranquility than some other societies do. I can't tell you how many times over the years I have said some version of this: "Oh my God, I'm 20 minutes away and the place closes in 15 and it's pouring rain and I just broke the heel off my shoe and if I don't turn this thing in today my life is over, can you lend me your umbrella, oh, never mind, I'll just get wet."

And my Costa Rican colleague, acquaintance, husband or other family member has said some version of: "OR, you could sit down for just a minute and have a *cafecito*, and wait for the rain to subside, and take a few deep breaths, and let's take a look at that shoe." It's as if the entire population, male and female, comes with a built-in maternal instinct. Calm down, dear. Let's figure this out.

But what if I don't get the thing to the place and the deadline expires and I can't fix my shoe? Well, then, *hagamos un MacGyver*.

That's right—MacGyver, the TV icon who could disarm a bomb with (insert random ingredients here, such as a tube of Pringles and a Nair facial wax strip), is highly revered in Costa Rica and has become a part of daily language. Stuck in traffic? *Hagamos un MacGyver* and we'll go the wrong way down this unused one-way street. Oops . . . the one-way street wasn't unused, but rather very much used by a large and uncompromising 18-wheeler? *Hagamos un MacGyver*, otherwise known as a lightning-quick U-turn up on the curb and through part of a garage. Something, anything at all really, is wrong with your car or home or life? There is a MacGyver to be done.

Your dad and I took the train home one night from the National Stadium after a game and got off near the university for a nightcap. It was a good thing we'd planned to do that, because when we alighted we saw that our train might not be going any farther anyway. Some yahoo had parked right on the tracks.

Now, I have never parked a car on train tracks in a major U.S. city, but I assume it would not end well. Either the train would plow right over it, or you'd get arrested and fined a zillion dollars, or both. But this was Costa Rica, and here was the car, and a train far too slow and clunky to pulverize it, and lots of people waiting to get home, and no apparent solution in sight.

Then the call went up: *Hagamos un MacGyver.* A dozen guys got off the train and started bouncing the car up and down, up and down, until it bounced so merrily that they were able to cajole it right off the tracks, as a happy crowd gathered around to watch. Five minutes later, the car was moved, the train lumbered forward, and all was well. This would never have occurred to me. I laughed out loud.

I thought about this again later when I was back in New York for a meeting. As I gazed forlornly at the plastic barrier dividing me from my taxi driver on my way to my hotel, I was just starting to think, *I miss Costa Rica, where you can almost always count on your* taxista *for an interesting chat*, when the driver turned around and asked me where I was coming in from that day. He turned out to be delightful and very interested in Costa Rica, which he had seen just that week on a TV show. Is it really full of volcanoes and jungle? Is it beautiful there? Are the people nice? (Yes. Yes. As nice as can be.)

As we neared Columbus Circle, we saw three fire trucks lined up. "Must be a big one," I said.

"No, no, NO! This country," he said, all but shaking his fist at the trucks as we lurched by. "I tell you what happens in this country. Someone drops a cigarette in a trash can here, it makes a little fire, everyone calls the firemen. You know what happens in Bangladesh? Someone throws a little water on the fire, POOSH! It's done."

I laughed, thinking: Costa Rica, all the way.

"The firemen in Bangladesh—they are never out," he went on, bursting with pride. "They sleep all year round. They go through the street once a year, just so you can see them. Rest of the time? Sleep."

Costa Rica, Costa Rica. I mean, I'm sure Costa Rican firefighters are very good, but the spirit was familiar. I wanted to tell the taxi driver about the concept of the MacGyver, one I am sure he would have appreciated, but we arrived at my hotel and that was that.

Later that same week, I received a product recall notice regarding the car seat I had bought for you in the United States a year or so earlier. "Oh, no," I thought as I opened it. "Is she in danger of being crushed, annihilated, strangled by manic buckles?"

Here is what it said: *This recall is due to food and dried liquids can make [sic] some harness buckles progressively more difficult to open over time or become stuck in the latched position. If a harness buckle becomes difficult to open or stuck in the latched position, a caregiver could be delayed from removing a child from a car seat in the event of an emergency.*

I mean. Really. What would MacGyver do? Get out a damp sponge, perhaps.

I wanted to buy a ticket to New York and find my taxi driver and show it to him. I thought about him up there in that towering city, watching TV in a little apartment, wondering about the volcanoes and jungles of Costa Rica, wistful for the drowsy firefighters of Bangladesh. I wish I had taken an extra ride around the block to tell him about the beauty of *un MacGyver*. Life, like certain taxi rides, goes by too fast.

At the end of the day, my dear, I think the reason that foreigners find life in Costa Rica to be saner and calmer than it was elsewhere is that we are surrounded by a cheerful, no-nonsense pragmatism and a belief that most things just aren't worth getting your panties in a twist, or missing your afternoon coffee, or going out in a downpour. When your boss and coworkers and all others around you encourage you to take it easy on yourself, your Puritan attitude starts to lose its sternness. I can imagine many unbelievably high-achieving Costa Ricans I know saying, "Ahhhh, but this nonchalance is also what keeps us from achieving so many things as a nation! This acceptance of mediocrity and procrastination has held our society back in myriad ways!" Which is also right, and only goes to show that, for a nation as for an individual, the worst qualities are often the best ones as well, and the best are also the worst.

I wouldn't wish for you a life free of hard work and stress—and I don't know anyone here who has such a life anyway, since some of the happiest Costa Ricans I know are the ones shouldering heavy burdens of work and even tragedy. I hope that, to paraphrase the Episcopal Bishop Gene Robinson, you'll one day be blessed with the tears, anger and discomfort one needs to feel in order to make a difference in the world. I hope you will worry about things that matter. I hope you'll get your homework in on time. But I'm glad you're also surrounded by a nation of mothers who'll urge you to value your own tranquility. I pray that Costa Rica grants you a merry, MacGyver-pulling soul.

October 25, 2005

My roommate is moving out. I am indecisive about everything, so I'm not sure how this happened, but when I told Adrián the news and he said, "Why don't I live here with you?" I felt the smile pull my whole face up toward the ceiling. Cartoon happiness. Why am I so certain after less than a year of dating? No idea. It's so unlike me.

    We had a party to celebrate, and then my roommate was gone, and Adrián was here with not much more than a box of books and a black plastic garbage bag full of clothes (yup, a garbage bag . . . welcome to living with a man). As our friends headed out the door we sat together on the bright-orange couch that came with the house, waving goodbye, like castaways on a very small and inordinately happy island.

N
AVE
WISDOM ON THE BUS

Dear E,

Every year of your life, we have spent one month in the States. We do it so you can see your grandparents, and so that I can remind myself—and you, I hope—where I come from. They now live by the water in Downeast Maine.

It is a place that operates on the rhythm of the sea and the ships that travel that sea. It is a place whose native residents look out on the bay, perhaps with fondness, but also with a practicality that is lost upon the tourists who see it only as a beautiful view, or hear in the foghorn only a convenient bit of ambiance, and think of rain only in terms of how it affects whale-watching plans. To those who make their lives in such a town, the sea is a determiner of fates and fortunes. Whether a ship comes into Eastport bearing scallops or sightseers, that cargo is precious to the businesses and families ashore. You can sense that everyone is attuned to the comings and goings of the vessels, the shade of the sky.

You and I don't know what that's like. When it comes to ships and boats and oceans, we are tourists all the way. I admire them from the pier with a nice hot coffee in my hand, gaze out over the water with the requisite far-off look in my eye, snuggle into my covers at night when I hear that cozy foghorn. You run along the shore, short legs whirring, racing the sails out at sea, or you jump up and down on the wooden dock, looking for billowing jellyfish in the dark water.

Where you and I live now, our ship, our *nave*, is a different type of craft. It creaks and wails just as much as a wooden vessel. It plows through waves on occasion, as optimistically and ill-advisedly as a tugboat in a storm. We, too, live in its rhythms, memorize its sounds and tricks and fickle schedules. But here in San José, the *nave* is not a ship. It is a bus.

Your dad, looking down the street to see his bus approaching, might say, "*Allí viene la nave*" —"there comes my boat." The first time I heard him say this, years ago, I was charmed, and I have thought of the city's buses that way ever since. They might not determine our fates and fortunes, but in a place where city bus schedules are virtually nonexistent, good or bad bus luck can certainly color your whole day. Most of us don't develop a personal relationship with a San José bus driver the way you might with the city's *taxistas*. However, you do come to recognize them, and when your bus pulls up at just the right moment—as you are clinging to groceries and a toddler in the pouring rain, for example—you are as grateful as a castaway boarding a luxurious cruise ship. You feel a deep, deep love for the curmudgeonly man driving the *Doña Xiomara*, or *Jesús es mi Salvador*, or whatever the painted letters on the side might proclaim.

My favorite bus, ridden once long before you were born and never found again, was a Zapote-to-San José vessel with a huge sign inside that said "I love my wife," with photos of this matronly personage and little felt hearts all over the windshield. There were even hearts on the standard foam coin-holder near the stick shift. I wondered whether the unsmiling driver was a secret romantic, or whether his wife had taken some precautionary measures to protect her spouse. This might have been justified, since I have been told that sometimes bus drivers attain groupies: women who hang out in the front seats and fawn over the all-powerful man at the wheel. I have yet to see a bus driver whose appearance seems to justify this status, but *gustos son gustos*—there's no accounting for taste.

Bus stories tend to be less vivid than taxi stories. Rather than being thrust into close proximity and intimate conversation with one stranger, you are dipping your toes into a river of humanity in a more detached way. If Heraclitus had been a bus rider, he might have pointed out that the water in that river changes—the faces and conversations around you switch, the buskers and the characters— but the fact is, it's always the same river. The people stand out in your bus memory not so much as individuals, but as types. The man selling lollipops who pulls up his shirt to show the terrible scar from the surgery that has made him unfit to work. The flocks of teenagers squawking over smartphones after school gets out, an event that can take place at virtually any time of day. The neat and friendly *abuelos y abuelas* who always seem to forgive the sullen riders refusing to give up their seat for the elderly, or pretending to be asleep so no one will take the window seat next to them. The English-speakers who are trying to figure out the stops and count their change, or those who show quiet competence and inevitably make me wonder what brought them here.

Then there are the captains of these unruly crews, who jostle their way through exhausting and repetitive journeys, day after day. They have their patterns, their tricks; they wave and honk at their colleagues passing the other way. They pick up their family members or friends who hop up the back steps so as not to register on the people-counter up front, or vault right over the metal bars. They allow certain buskers while not others.

Sometimes they'll surprise you. One driver, just the other day, stopped the bus in the middle of a busy street, got off, and disappeared. I have lived here long enough to know that he was probably picking up lunch or a snack, but I couldn't see where he might have gone, and he was gone for a while.

"Where is the MAN?" you asked me. I realized you and I were the only people on the bus. I contemplated moving up front and driving the bus on home, alone.

"That's a good question," I told you. "But get used to this."

He returned eventually, clutching the classic Styrofoam-boxed *casado*, and the bus groaned on up the hill.

Riding the bus has its moments, and I can't imagine getting to know San José without it. That said, if I never had to take a bus again, especially during a steamy rainy-season rush hour, I would be perfectly content. (You, little daughter, would not agree: you clearly believe that every time you step onto one, you are entering a party at which every guest was invited for your own personal delight.) This is why I have started keeping running clothes and shoes at my office, an escape hatch on those days when the commute home seems too daunting.

This past Friday, photos of flooded streets in downtown San José popped up all over Twitter, causing everyone in my office to shiver with fear at the thought of the trips that awaited us. I looked out at the rain coming down, changed my clothes and shoes, wrapped my wallet and phone in plastic before stashing them in my small backpack, and headed out. I stepped into a vertical wave. I was instantly drenched to the bone. I am as slow as can be, but as I ran past the cars lurching out of our parking lot, I felt like The Flash. I felt like a kid.

Squelching with every step, but faster and freer than any ship, I set out alone, swimming for shore.

December 17, 2005

I finally met Adrián's family, in the best and scariest way possible. He threw me straight into the lion's den yesterday by taking me to a tamaleada. *In theory, this meant I was going to participate in the complex, family-wide event of preparing Christmas tamales, which are pork and vegetables encased in ground-corn dough, wrapped in banana leaves and boiled to steamy perfection. In practice, it meant that I was given the task of wrapping and tying up the tamales, and made a small pile of terribly misshapen ones before I was gently relieved of my task and sent to have a cup of coffee in the corner. I think it might have been a genius move to meet his family this way, since I was too distracted by string and knots to get too nervous.*

I understand about half of what is being said at any given time, especially by Adrián. He is different around his family. In my life, he is a calm and steady presence, but within his family he is in constant motion, verbally more than physically. He seems to have a comeback for every line in a conversation, generally unintelligible to me but whose meaning can be approximated by the guffaws and screeches and eye rolls they elicit. Throughout our relationship I've lamented the fact that my natural sarcasm in English doesn't translate. I suddenly realize he's had the same handicap. I speak Spanish, but not his *Spanish.*

Most of his family lives within a three-block radius. My own family is scattered across the globe like dandelion fluff. I can't even imagine what this kind of geographic closeness would be like. Can I borrow a cup of sugar? Could you come over and help me move my sofa? Wonderful, comfortable, impossible.

OF MAES AND MEN

Dear E,

I may be getting a little ahead of myself, since you haven't yet learned how to put on socks, but here are a few thoughts on relationships—in case they still exist when you are an adult and have not yet become an app of some kind. (Here you'll say, "App? Man, she is SO OLD.")

At the heart of Costa Rican language and, in many ways, the heart of the way your father talks, is the word "*mae.*" A little like "man" (as in "hey, man"), a little like "dude" (in a certain time and place), with complex origins and rules of use I won't get into here, it is the way many Costa Rican men—and some women, in specific contexts—address each other. I call your dad *El Mae*, or *El Mejor Mae que Hay*. Before you were born, we called you *la maecilla*. The word *mae* is actually engraved inside my wedding ring, as a bit of a joke. I kept trying to think of something unique and meaningful to put in there, something that would capture the feel of us in a few characters. When the woman behind the counter, probably a bit exasperated, told me that I could always just put your dad's initials, I smiled and thought, "That's it!" I gave her three letters, as she suggested: M.A.E.

The thing with *mae* is that when your dad, like a lot of Ticos, really gets going, he can fit it into a single sentence about ten times. I noticed this when we first started dating and we'd get into a taxi. *"Mae, a Vargas, mae, pero subimos por Sabanilla, mae, entrando por el antiguo Gallo Pinto, mae."* I loved it. One night, I made fun of this, and instantly regretted it. All he said was, "Oh," but the next time we got into a taxi, his instructions were *mae*-less. I felt awful. Over a period of weeks, I was able to reinstate the reign of *mae* in our lives. When he talks to your uncle about Saprissa, their mutually beloved soccer club, it's a popcorn of *mae*s, the way it should be.

I was thinking about my *mae* misstep recently, and it made me realize two things. First: In a bicultural, binational relationship, the person who gets to live in his or her native country doesn't always have the upper hand. Sure, I go on and on about being the foreigner, about having to deal with homesickness and awkwardness and not always understanding what's going on—but I also get to remain the expert on my own background and language. How are things done in the United States? Well, let me tell you. How is that said in English? Allow me to expound. There's no one around to contradict me, because no one else in this house has lived in my homeland, and yet I get to analyze Costa Rica all I want. There is no one here to correct or comment on the way I speak English—at least, until you get a bit older and start to correct everything I do— but I get to opine on the number of *mae*s in a sentence.

At any rate, while the best advice I ever received about marriage was not to keep score, I do believe that in the mathematics of a cross-border relationship, we may be more even than we think. One of us is at home, but over time, the other comes to be at home in two places at once, which is another kind of power.

The second thing I realized was more general, and this is what I really want to tell you. It's how vulnerable the people we love really are when they are with us. No matter how serene and confident and calm people might seem, how much older and wiser they might be, we are all babies underneath. We are toddling around on fat little legs hoping for a pat on the head. Unless we are unusually toughened by terrible circumstances, we are so easily hurt, so quickly bruised. When it comes to the people we trust the most, a careless putdown can shake the very *maes* from our sentences.

It is a little easier for me to remember this now, when I have you running through my life in a diaper and covered with magic marker, tossing Cheerios into the universe wherever you go, but I hope I will remember it always, and I hope you will remember it too: that even as husbands or wives, partners or friends, *maes* or men, we are babies first and foremost. We live best when we treat each other the way we would if we really understood that every day. That is to say, with reverence, with respect, with a careful, almost breathless love.

May 8, 2006

Feet up, sore. My first Costa Rican Inauguration Day. I spent approximately seven billion hours waiting for Laura Bush at a public elementary school—seven billion, because the Secret Service found a teacher's drawer they couldn't unlock, and couldn't bring in the First Lady until that teacher was located somewhere in town and arrived to unlock it. When Mrs. Bush finally did arrive, she smiled at the room, watched a group of carefully combed children do something cute, said something about the importance of reading, and was whisked off to the presidential ceremony. That's the thing about reporting, I've learned. The things that sound fancy, you could write them without even going.

And the things that sound straightforward can surprise you. On election night back in February, I stood in a crowd at a random intersection in San Pedro outside the Citizen Action Party headquarters. I expected to get some comments from the also-ran, jot down some details for color, and cover a concession speech, but the numbers kept rolling in and the crowd grew more and more excited. Costa Rica has been a two-party country for decades, and Citizen Action is not one of those parties. Was this history in the making, an upset no pollster saw coming? My phone rang nonstop as reporters at hotel conference rooms around the city compared notes and then called in the details to our newsroom.

At around two in the morning, Adrián came down the hill from our house to join me. Finally, we realized this wouldn't be resolved in one night (it would last a month, in fact). We got a burger and went home. In the taxi, sending off a few last texts as my friends called it quits as well, I thought: this is what I'll miss someday.

P

A' LA CHOZA

GOING HOME

Dear E,

I slip out of the house into the cool evening. It's late-summer twilight in New England, God's attempt at justice for those who live in cold climates. These endless sunsets that stretch long past dinner make it possible to end the day with a run—a luxury impossible in Costa Rica, where the sun drops like a dead weight at six-ish, year-round. (I know, I know. I can feel the wrathful eyes of Mainers upon me. I'm not complaining, and yes, I know I haven't scraped the ice off a car in 15 years. But you know it as well as I do—a Maine summer, for all its brevity, is perfection.)

I've got a good hour of light left, but it's dim enough that the living-room window looks cozy as I pass it, and I pause, torn, reluctant to turn away. Inside, two heads lean together, conferring in front of the record player, your grandmother's gray, yours brown, both equally tousled. A Sesame Street record starts to play. I make myself keep going down the driveway and into the street. Goodbye for now, *mi choza*, I think. *Choza*, one of the first words your father taught me. Literally a hut made of palms, but also a comfortable slang word for home. This home is *mi choza gringa*, my stateside place to hang my hat.

I'm not from this town, which has always made visits particularly luxurious. I never run into a former crush at the coffee shop or a hated teacher at the hair salon. There are only good memories here. Your dad's first glimpse of snow. Our quiet, joyful wedding at your grandmother's church. Fleeting, perfect family reunions. Your first steps on U.S. soil. August evenings like this one, cool, almost crisp, edging toward autumn.

My feet turn toward my favorite route, around the block and down the hill toward a farmhouse I love. As I run, I realize that while I'm not from this place, or anyplace, really, I am from the things that surround me at this moment. I am from the soft colors of New England, rather than tropical brights: weathered farmhouse red, muffled summer yellows and oranges, palest green lichens on stone walls, blues of distant hills. I am from the sweet smell of cut grass. I am from the local meeting I pass in the old stone jail-house-turned-library, where high-backed wooden chairs stand in a half-circle in the warm lamplight, your grandfather among the attendees, glimpsed as I run past. I am from wide fields and the sound of crickets and dry leaves in the ditches. I am from cemeteries with thin, crooked headstones. I am from these lean woods, full of leggy birches, spacious and tall even in the lushness of summer, with soft red needles below.

At one point, the beauty around me slows my legs like molasses and roots me to the spot. I look at the pink-gray clouds, the open fields, and am at home. It might not be my hometown, but I know these stones and skies. This isn't a place I learned to love, like San José—this is a place I love without thinking.

But both kinds of love have their role to play. I reach the farm and find that the sun is finally setting, blazing across the flat, still waters of the farm's ponds. There's fire among the rushes, a willow turned to gold. I loop down to the driveway and turn back, and the moment is gone. That slow summer sun disappeared quickly, in the end, just as it does in Costa Rica.

Time's up. *Jale pa' la choza.* I push up the long hill, wistful. As I run, I tell myself that I can take it all with me, that home is no longer a place or even a country. It's the colors and smells and sounds I remember. Even as I think this, I'm not sure it's true, but one thing I do know: for now, and as far into the future as I care to imagine, *mi choza* is wherever you are.

August 21, 2006

I put my hand in my pocket yesterday as I waited to cross the street. I'd felt something clinking there, and my fingers found a mass of small coins, light and thin and barely enough to cool the skin. U.S. coins. It's funny how fast I slide back into the clunkety bus, the beans and rice, the heavy coins.

Adrián and I just spent a week and a half in Maine and Boston, his first trip to the States and my whole family's first time meeting him. It went by too fast. At the Museum of Fine Arts, walking in and thinking about tired feet, I asked which section he most wanted to see. He said, "Everything." And we did. As closing time approached, we were practically sprinting, which is how I felt about the whole vacation. I always feel that way when I'm back in the States: when you could happily spend four or five hours in a CVS or Target, there will never be enough hours in any day. On this trip, however, it was particularly true.

I was so nervous about his getting a visa so he could go with me. It was a long shot, since he is unmarried without any property, and we were thrilled when it was approved—no thanks at all to the binder full of forms and papers we had painstakingly prepared, which seemed to matter not a whit. It felt like the U.S. Consulate had in its hands the entire future of our relationship, and in a way, it did, because being able to go home with Adrián at my side seemed essential. It made the relationship real. It made it whole, filled in the blanks: I had seen his high school and met his sisters and cousins, but it took this week for my past to catch up. It was surreal and somehow very normal to see him among the old familiar things at my parents' house, playing tennis at their local high school, strolling around Harvard Square.

Maybe we can make this work somehow. Here? There? In a Boston brownstone with a secret passageway that pops up in the Plaza de la Cultura? I don't know, but now it all seems a little more feasible than before.

Qué Baldazo

WHY MOTHERHOOD IS BETTER IN THE RAIN

Dear E,

The rainy season with you is lonely and cozy. We live in a city, and in summer it feels that way—we hear footfalls back and forth, one neighbor shouting to another, a conversation outside our gate, a honk for a friend, soccer *oooooh*s from the bar down the hill. In the rain, though, with your dad out working at the restaurant, our house becomes a ship's cabin in the middle of the ocean. Watching you walk around like a tiny, drunken sailor serves to heighten the effect; I'm the only one here with sea legs. As I write this, a torrential rain has been falling for six hours straight. You are finally down for the night. I patted you to sleep, watched your eyes drop shut like magic over a count of ten.

Yes, the winter is quiet and hushed, particularly because once the rain begins, it hushes one of the country's loudest and most notable sounds. It was a sound I first encountered at, oh, three in the morning, in the days before you made that a perfectly normal time for me to get up.

"What is that damned *noise*?" I asked your father, on whom the incredible din outside our window seemed to have absolutely no effect.

"The national bird of Costa Rica," he murmured, his pride waking up even before he did.

"The national what?"

In response, he uttered a sequence of vowels that were unintelligible to me at the time, but which I know in retrospect must have been "*yigüirro.*"

"Why is it making so much noise at night?"

"*Está pidiendo agua,*" he explained, and rolled over, end of discussion. It's asking for water. It's asking for rain.

Costa Rica is home to any number of spectacular, jaw-dropping birds, but it's not the scarlet macaw or gorgeous toucan or lovely motmot who's calling the shots: it's the clay-colored thrush, a plain brown bird whose unremarkable appearance is matched by its unfortunate scientific name, *Turdus grayi.* I like to think that Costa Rica's choice of the *yigüirro* reflects the country's practical nature. Surrounded by so much feathered beauty, they went with the bird that knows what's going on. They say that *una golondrina no hace verano* (one swallow does not a summer make), but Costa Rica does have a single bird who makes winter. At least, that's how it feels.

Every year as summer winds down and the rains approach, like clockwork, much more reliable than any groundhog, the *yigüirro* and its unique song "ask for rain." María Mayela Padilla writes in *Dichos y Refranes de los Ticos* that according to one veterinarian she consulted, the birds actually sing at this time of year because it's their time to mate—but she goes on to say that surely they are also yearning for water as folklore suggests, because the birds look so content when the rain does arrive and they splash around in the puddles.

While I've made a happy avocation of listening to the words on Costa Rican lips, one of the sounds that would remind me of Costa Rica most quickly, years and miles hence, wouldn't be human at all. It'd be the unmistakable, slightly spooky annual reports of the country's best weathermen.

There's a whole host of things a foreigner must learn when it comes to Costa Rican weather. First and foremost, we must learn that rain is not necessarily rain. I once went to a conference in Toronto and, when it ended, arranged with a Panamanian colleague to split a cab from our hotel to the airport. On the morning of our departure, she called my room to ask whether we should leave earlier than planned. "I checked the forecast, and it says it's going to rain," she said. I glanced out the window at a nondescript, heavy, gray day, and told her no, we'd left plenty of wiggle room. Later, as our taxi pulled away from the curb, a light rain was falling.

"I thought it was going to rain," she said, gazing out toward the CN Tower.

"It *is* raining," I said.

"This?" She was shocked. "This isn't rain! Come on, now."

I burst out laughing, not at her, but at myself, for forgetting. How many times have your father and I had the same conversation? "*Está lloviendo*," I'll say, it's raining, and he'll correct me. This isn't rain. It's hair of the cat (*pelo de gato*), or *llovizna*, or *está garruando*. Actual *lluvia*, in a tropical country, is a serious affair. Rain means that every pothole or crevice in sight—that is, thousands— overflows. Rain means that the umbrella you optimistically hold overhead keeps water away from your face, but not from the rest of your body, because sheets of water are blowing in horizontally. Rain is a plans-changer, a traffic-stopper, a car-swamper, a water-oozing-down-your-walls *event*. It's an *aguacero* or a *chaparrón* or even a *baldazo*—a bucketful. So when a Costa Rican gazes skyward and tells you, "*Está de agua*," or "*Se puso de agua*," or "*Ya viene el agua*," I've learned to pay attention, 'cause things are about to get real. I've also learned that when I hear "*Se vino la doña de los *frescos*"—literally, "The lady who sells drinks is here"—I should grab my umbrella, not my milk money.

Costa Rica may have only two seasons, differentiated by factors that, to a person used to ice storms and leaf piles and dog days, might seem slight. But those two seasons don't mess around. Not only does rain come by the bucketful, but the seasons also come and go with panache, like divas given a dull script but determined to bring it to life through sheer force of will. Summer goes out with intense heat that leaves you gasping, droughts that leave the Guanacaste plains a spiky brown. Winter leaves you drowning by degrees in endless umbrella puddles, fantasizing about afternoon walks and Christmas breezes. What's more, both seasons, while sashaying out the door, throw in some apocalyptic events for good measure. Mild-mannered birds wake you up in the night. Little earthquakes abound as climate patterns shift (according to popular belief, at least) as if to toss us into the next season by the scruffs of our necks. Everyone gets terrible colds: "Ah, it's the change of the weather," the pharmacist will say. Volcanic ash is falling? Seems par for the course. I wouldn't be that surprised if frogs or locusts showed up, too.

I miss autumn. I miss long summer nights and hot cocoa after snow and the first shoots of spring. But I've found that learning another weather is just like learning another language, with the same broadening of perspective, the same opening of the soul. It's humbling to be instructed in the specific amount of precipitation that constitutes *pelo de gato*. It's satisfying to feel the coming of a real *aguacero*. It's comforting to find familiarity in what was once very foreign: the expressions that capture a particular feel of water on skin. The phrases that connote the sound of a storm coming at you in the city. The birdsong that tells the story, without any words at all, of the ominous press of heat, the heaviness of clouds, the silence of a country at night, waiting for a change.

Of course, I don't need to tell you this. You are a child of the rainy season, of hair of the cat and its more forceful cousins. You were two months old when the most dramatic thunderstorm I can remember raged around our house. You were feeding, and flinched at each crack of thunder, your whole body and your small, wincing face burrowing into my chest. It may have been the only time in your life that rain will truly surprise you. Already, you are used to the downpour, and so am I. I love it. I wait for the rainy season eagerly, and wish it gone only during months six and seven (whereupon I wish it gone with every fiber of my being and crave sun, dry shoes, and open-air happy hours).

There are many words for rain, but it can also be called simply water. One day, just about the time I was trying to come to terms with the idea that we might never get to have kids after all, your father and I walked up the hill to the nicer neighborhood, the one with the slanty park and quiet streets and view of San José. It was gray and hushed. Suddenly he grabbed my hand. Look, he said. "*Ya viene el agua.*" Here comes the water. It's really the best way to describe rain that is more than rain: it's a flying river, a vertical ocean, a flash flood. We stood there, looking out over our city, watching a wall of tiny drops, a gray line in the distance, sweep toward us over rusty tin roofs. It was astonishing. When rain is that dramatic, you don't even mind being soaked to the bone.

Ya viene el agua. And so it came, bringing you on its back.

March 1, 2007

Argh. Another long night, sleepless hours spent on the orange couch, agonizing. There is an engagement ring on my finger, but my brain hasn't caught up. I sit there in the living room night after night, looking around at it: not a stick of the furniture is mine. Not a shred of this existence was meant to be permanent. Am I ready to make it so? This city, these buses, this traffic, these bookstores where all the books are shrink-wrapped and you can't browse, this separation from my family, all the things that fall onto the "hate" side of the wobbly love-hate tightrope walk?

On the other hand, am I ready to inflict that experience on the man who is sleeping so peacefully in the other room? Am I ready to take a person who is Costa Rican to his bones and throw him into a totally different existence? He says, absolutely, we can move to the States anytime; that's part of the deal. He is willing to do that for me, but am I willing to do that to him? I imagine him shoveling snow, dreaming of good coffee and limey, salty Tronaditas, trying to figure out how to stream a Saprissa game in some apartment in Boston or Portland, and my heart fails me—almost literally. Or that's how it feels.

The other day I poured this out to my parents on the phone, ending with something like, "I'm just so confused!" and my dad said, "Of course you are! You fell in love with a Costa Rican." It was one of those comments that stops you mid-sentence. I knew just what he meant: Who said this would be easy? This is what you signed up for. You can go left, or you can go right, but this is the crossroads you picked. And if you choose him, this split existence, then these yearnings and distances will be the geography of your life.

It's nearly dawn. I can hear the first bus of the day coming down the hill.

R

EQUETEFURRIS

MY SAN JOSE TRAFFIC FANTASY

Dear E,

You were conceived in the middle of a San José rush hour.

All right, that's a lie. (Did I make you throw up a little there? I'm sorry.) But even if you weren't, someone must have been. Think about it. This is a city where an enterprising, or perhaps very bored, reporter wandered around on foot last year during *la hora pico,* as this daily ordeal is known, interviewing exasperated drivers through their car windows. When he came back around the block and recognized the same drivers, he did some quick calculations and realized that they were moving at a rate of one kilometer per hour. That's right: one kilometer per *hour.*

In urban sludge that thick, people do lots of things to pass the time. They straighten their hair, buy the cell-phone covers and roses proffered by strolling salespeople, watch movies on the DVD players they have installed on their windshields in a special affront to road safety, perform root canals, make five-course dinners on dashboard hot plates. It stands to reason that people must be taking advantage of the proximity of a totally immobile back seat, plus a spouse, or carpool member, or perhaps a passing pedestrian who, compared to the cars, is moving at the speed of LIGHT and therefore seems inordinately powerful and attractive and worthy of a spontaneous shag.

This entry is not particularly appropriate for my little daughter's innocent ears, and it's not going to improve; better save this one until you're 50 or so. Because I have to tell you that my definition of a San José resident is a person who fantasizes about urban planning instead of sex. I am absolutely serious. It's worse during the rainy season, when your bus or taxi is like a sauna because the windows have to stay up, and your pants or skirt or socks or all of the above are sopping wet, and you're going the wrong way up a steep one-way street the width of a bike lane because it's the only way your *taxista* can figure to get around this one nasty spot, but you're at a standstill anyway because fifty other cars and a horse trailer had the same idea, and you would rather rip your eyeballs out with your fingers than sit in the traffic for one. More. Minute.

I could write multiple epic novels about San José traffic—to be read aloud during mealtimes in hell—but suffice it to say that at times like this, a gorgeous figure leaps into my mind. He resembles Gandhi, but is wearing fatigues (bear with me here) and is extremely buff. He has to be, because he is hoisting Wile E. Coyote-style barrels of TNT above both shoulders. That's just how I picture the benevolent despot who would have to seize power in Costa Rica in order to fix the traffic situation, but who, after sorting things out, would hand power back over and allow democracy to resume. He stares at me and addresses me in the voice of Barry White:

Me: What are you going to do for me first?

Gandhi/Barry: Baby, first I'm gonna dynamite the Outlet Mall and the surrounding three blocks and build an east-side terminal to reduce bus traffic in San José.

Me: Ooh, that's right. Right there. And can a shard from the blast kill the guy with the whistle who keeps the buses lined up on the other side of the street to block the intersection for no reason so people can't make a right turn?

Gandhi/Barry: Absolutely. I'll name my cross-town elevated bullet train after him. Then I'll vaporize everyone who texts while driving, thereby reducing the population by approximately 72%, and turn all the roundabouts into four-way intersections with proper computerized traffic lights.

Me: Oh, God. Yes. Don't stop.

Fortunately for San José, the Spanish language is full of delightful words for messes, turning disasters into poetry. French may be the language of love and English the language of business, but Spanish is the language to turn to when you're screwed, disorganized, pissed off, or ass over tincups. There's "*desmadre*," "*despelote*," "*despiche*," "*lío*," and the eloquent "*cagada*," a big ol' crap. I still remember how overjoyed I was when I first heard the phrase "*cagar en la olla de leche*," to crap in the pot of milk, a description so vivid that it makes me want to screw up just so I can say it.

My favorite, though, is "*furris*." I don't know where this comes from, but I find that "*estar furris*"—to be up Shit Creek without a paddle, as your grandfather has been known to say—is a satisfying phrase. It makes me think of a happy, furry little puppy, yet also captures the feel of the giant, hairy, horrible mess that is crossing this city at five o'clock on a Friday. Not to mention a Friday that's also a payday. Or a Friday close to Mother's Day. Or a Friday when it's raining, or when it might rain, or when there is a soccer game sometime in the next month. You know how it is. *Estamos furris.* If something's really terrible, you can even add the prefix *re-* (*refurris*) or *requete-* (*requetefurris*). If you ever have to go from Santa Ana to Cartago in late afternoon on a major Christmas shopping day, those are the words to use.

My dear, I so fervently hope that, should you live in this city when you're bigger, it will have found a way to a less furry existence. Your beloved Chepe and lovely Costa Rica deserve so much better. But I fear that you, too, will someday hear Barry White's voice in your mind as you sit in the back of a taxi. Unless taxis fly by the time you read this. In which case, I sincerely hope I'm already dead.

I like to end these little essays with something positive. It's hard to come up with anything in this case, since the spectacular gridlock is certainly the worst part of living here. The one good thing I can say about it is that it led me to motherhood: the only way I could think of to get myself out of all these godawful traffic jams was to procreate so I'd be forced to work from home. I did, and it changed my life. I've only been in three or four really terrible traffic jams in the past couple years, and that's all because of you. So thanks. You were born for the sole purpose of saving your mother from *la hora pico*.

All right, that's a lie. But even if you weren't, someone must have been.

April 22, 2007

Life course resolved by volcanic gases.

Adrián and I took a Holy Week trip to Río Celeste, so named because the gases from nearby volcanoes give its water an opaque blue color. Like many things worth seeing in this country, it requires a long drive that ends on a tooth-rattling dirt road, and then a bit of a hike. We finally got to the banks of the Sky-Blue River and it was officially brown.

A park guard told us that rains had been muddying the water, but I was heartbroken out of all proportion. In this quest to decide whether to get married, I have searched for signs everywhere, and this seemed like a bad one.

At our cabin that night I wondered whether this was just another adventure in our lives together, or the last one. At one point I stepped outside and gazed into the blackness. I could picture myself telling our kids about the time we went to Río Celeste and I was so unsure about marrying their dad. I could also picture myself telling an entirely different family about the time I almost lived the rest of my life in Costa Rica before I came to my senses and headed home. They always say there's a moment where doubt falls away: I thought maybe I would never have one. Maybe I would never say, the way people do, "And that was that!"

The next morning Adrián said, "Let's go back to the river before we head home." Ugh—I didn't want to. That drive again, that hike. But we did, and by the time we started the hike I was in tears. Full-on, psychotic sobbing as we walked along the trail. No idea why, and every idea.

I don't believe in signs, but goddamit, that river was blue.

We took a few pictures of each other at the base of the waterfall, gazed at the otherworldly color, crouched in the quiet. For some reason I can't explain, I was finished worrying. And that was that.

SIEMPRE ATRÁS COMO LOS HUEVOS DEL CHANCHO

THE KEY TO SPEAKING SPANISH

Dear E,

Usually, I aspire to examine Costa Rican language and culture with as much subtlety and sensitivity as I can muster. Usually, I hope that my bumbling travels through this linguistic wonderland are conducted with some modicum of class and grace.

But not today.

Today, I'm getting down to business—because at some point, you've just got to grab the Spanish language by the *huevos*. I'm sorry, but it has to be done, because if you live in Costa Rica, you might sometimes yearn for sharp cheddar cheese or real maple syrup, but you will never, ever want for eggs, whether in your kitchen or in the language you hear every day. And our family dictionary just wouldn't be complete without an eggy tangent, over easy.

The sale of eggs on the streets of Costa Rica is infinite, and infinitely annoying; when I watched the film *El Regreso* in the theater, a rant about *el mae que vende huevos* got the biggest laugh of the night. I don't know about wealthy enclaves or rural areas, but on many run-of-the-mill San José streets, the blissful silence of early morning is splintered daily by horrendous calls of "*¡Huevos huevos huevos huevos! ¡Llegaron los huevos!*" We're talking megaphones and pre-recorded messages blaring from battered old sedans where soon-to-expire eggs bounce along in the hot sun all morning. At some points over the past decade, there have been three egg cars on our street every single day, each selling eggs in packages of 30, which makes me wonder who is eating them all. Is a 500-pound man hiding in one of these little houses? Is there an NFL defensive line boarding with the nice old lady across the way?

Who knows, but it's fitting that there are eggs practically rolling down the streets, because they are a central part not only of Costa Rica's diet, but also its language. The word "*huevos*," of course, has a secondary, anatomical meaning that is pretty central to the use of Spanish in any informal setting. There are some equivalent expressions in English: We say, "It takes balls to drive in Boston," just as you need *huevos* to drive in San José; we say that someone is "ballsy," or that someone needs to "strap on a pair," and other versions of this. But in Spanish, the nuances and iterations are seemingly endless and pretty much ubiquitous. You, my daughter, will probably learn them all and then use them against me. But for the benefit of your family back in the United States, here is a primer.

Some phrases are obvious. You can *ponerle huevos*—be courageous, stand up for something. You can *hacerle huevo*—get the job done. You can have a *dolor de huevos*, which is, well, a real pain. But then there's *huevón*, or *güevón*, which begins to lead us into the untranslatable neighborhoods of egg linguistics. "*Huevón*" can be a commonplace greeting among male friends, or it can be a description of someone who is lazy, stubborn, a pain. The latter usage is often accompanied by a two-handed cupping gesture, of course, and the energy with which that gesture is made conveys the degree of annoyance. *Qué huevón ese mae. Qué señora más huevona.* And so on. Your grandpa, born and raised in Guatemala, used almost no Spanish with me when I was growing up except the word "*huevona*," which I got used to hearing whenever I was particularly lazy or frustrating. Along with a few other unprintables, it was my first foray into Spanish, which probably explains a lot.

Then there's "*ahuevado/a*," a fantastic and singularly expressive word. To be *ahuevado/a* is to be bummed out, down, done. Its perfect pronunciation still eludes me—it is basically a puff of vowels with the tiniest differentiation between the two "w" sounds of the *h* and *v*—but its "wah-wah" sound is the perfect accompaniment to the emotion it expresses. The word can also describe the event or situation that has made you feel that way. For example, a dull party can be *ahuevada*, or when you hear your friend describe a frustrating situation, "*Qué ahuevada, mae*" is the perfect response.

Finally, there's the king of them all, the number one phrase I am often lost without when speaking English: *manda huevo*. I can explain how it's used, but not why it means what it means. From what I can gather, it is quite rude in many Latin American countries, but while it's still uncouth in Costa Rica, it's also very useful. It can mean something close to "come on!" or "for crying out loud!" or "seriously?" As in, "What? You forgot to buy milk after I reminded you 50 times? *Manda huevo.*" It can mean "That's so unfair." For example: "I cooked this whole meal and you can't even clear the dishes? *Manda huevo.*" (Yes, it has lots of matrimonial applications.) Or, in its nicest version, it can express "But of course, it's the least I can do." As in, "Please, you don't need to thank me for giving you a ride home after you painted my whole house for free. *Manda huevo.*"

I'll tell you what really *me ahueva*. If the rating system for annoying noises is one to ten, one being an insistently clicking pen and ten being Fran Drescher, then two of the egg men who frequent our street rate a five or so. The third guy rates a fifty. He doesn't use a recording, which at least has the virtue of predictability. He cranks his megaphone as high as it will go and screams in a grating, piercing voice. I don't understand why anyone ever buys his eggs, but God help you if you ever do it and then stop, because then what he does is park outside your home every single morning at six o'clock and scream your name. That's why I've never given him a piece of my mind. Without any doubt, from now to eternity, he would park in front of our house daily and yell, *"Griiiiiiiiiiiinga. Griiiiiiiiinga. Gringagringagringagringa,"* or something much worse. No one wants to mess with the guy with all the eggs.

But someday, I swear I'll find some *huevos* of my own. I'll run out to his car and rip his megaphone from the roof. I'll grab his disease-ridden, heat-addled eggs and crack them into the megaphone's horn (since this is my imagination, he will somehow be unable to intervene until the whole thing is chock-full of a nasty soup). I'll then dunk his head in there like a thuggish high school bully until he limps away, nauseated, unable to stand the sight of megaphones or eggs for the rest of his life, one menace to society who will no longer roam the streets.

In this fantasy, my neighbors, who have emerged from their homes in awe, will break into a slow clap. I'll nod in a humble yet noble way, brush the eggshells from my hands, and take a dignified victory stroll through this hard-won kingdom of peace and harmony; you'll toddle right behind me, thinking proudly, "That's my mom!" As I pass the little cluster of men who always stand and talk in front of the *pulpería*, I'll overhear their conversation despite myself.

"Mae, esa gringa sí tiene huevos," someone will say admiringly.

"Pues sí, huevón."

"It was about time for somebody to *ponerle huevos* and take care of that *hij%&#$%&.*"

"Pues sí, mae, qué mae más huevón."

The *pulpero* will gaze reverently at my retreating figure. "I should do something for that inspiring and selfless woman. Maybe a lifetime supply of eggs?"

"Of course, *mae*. That, and maybe a statue."

"Diay, sí," they'll all say in unison. *"Manda huevo."*

July 21, 2007

Three years in Costa Rica today. Wedding preparations, happiness, much too little time with Adrián these days, since he works nights and weekends. He's at work now, cooking escargot or searing a steak or cleaning the kitchen or waiting for customers. Meanwhile, the country is getting ready for a historic referendum in which it will vote for or against a regional free-trade agreement with the United States. I've probably written 200 stories about it, but suddenly, I'm feeling nervous about the vote. I guess what's changing is that more and more, I've got skin in this game.

I am not reporting on it, either, which feels weird. I started a new job last month as a presidential assistant, which is the way life here seems to work sometimes: I went to a press conference one day as usual at Casa Presidencial and ran into the president's English communications adviser in the hallway. He mentioned he was going back to the States shortly and his job was opening up. A few months later I had packed up my desk at the paper and moved into the Office of the President, where I have been sorting letters, drafting documents, and keeping an interested eye on all the comings and goings. It looks like the president may give me a chance to work on one of his education initiatives, which would be a dream come true.

Each day, unbelievable opportunities are mixed with minutiae. A colleague tossed some letters across the desk to me that I would need to answer. One of them was signed by Bill Clinton; I spit-tested the signature and it looked real.

"Bill Clinton signed this letter, I think!" I said, all but jumping across the desk.

"Wow," said the staffer. "If that really excites you, you're going to love *this job."*

TAXISTAS

A LOVE STORY

Dear E,

My decade in Costa Rica has been guided, sustained, and enlivened by a long-term relationship spanning almost the entire period. Like most any relationship, it's had its ups and downs, but it's also been there for me through thick and thin, through rainstorms and heartbreak. As February, the month of love, came to a close, I found myself reflecting on ten years of heart-to-hearts and steadfast friendship.

Oh, I'm sorry. Did you think I was talking about your dad? I could say any of those things about him, too, but I'm referring here to my friends the *taxistas*: the armchair (or driver's-seat) philosophers and politicians, the distinguished and the mulleted, the reserved and the jovial. They've held my hand—figuratively speaking, of course—through many a learning curve, and taught me almost as many *dichos*, *refranes* and obscure street addresses as your father himself.

My love for *taxistas* is not universal. You roll the dice whenever you close one of those oh-so-fragile red doors (don't ever, ever slam them, as I learned on Day One!), just as they roll the dice when picking up a new client. There's plenty not to love: the *reggaetoneros* who slouch way down under the weight of their chains and scoot so far back that no one can sit behind them without yogic contortion; the ones who call their entire families, text incessantly, or watch movies while driving; the ones who act as though they have a personal vendetta against everyone else on the road, which they very well might; the ones who sigh as if you're asking them to break a hundred-dollar bill when you provide ₡2,000 for a ride costing ₡1,500.

Rather memorably, there was the guy who, as the cab pulled away into the street, said, "Thank God you hailed my taxi just now. You saved me from going to jail this very night."

An opening line like that one requires an answer, so I obliged. "Oh, yes? How's that?"

He explained that when I flagged him down, he had been on the way to murder his boss. (If you think this should have prompted me to ask to be let out of the taxi at once, you clearly haven't spent much time in downtown San José.) Apparently, the taxi driver and his wife of 15 years had five children, the youngest of whom had a congenital disease and desperately needed a special formula. He had asked his boss to pay him his salary just two days early so he could buy the formula and save his baby's life, but the coldhearted taxi mafioso refused. I didn't believe him, but found the story impressive enough that at the end of the ride I gave him a little extra "for your son." It was worth every *colón* when, a month later, I found myself once more in the same driver's taxi. He clearly didn't recognize me.

"Thank God you hailed my taxi just now," he said. "You saved me from going to jail this very night."

"I did?" I asked in amazement. "Tell me more!" I enjoyed myself immensely, stringing him along throughout rush-hour traffic that would otherwise have been interminable, before finally observing that it was very strange that the baby who one month earlier had been a three-month-old boy, was now a two-month-old girl, and that his five children had become three. I suggested that a man with such a cruel boss and, apparently, multiple wives and disappearing children, might want to stop procreating quite so vigorously. We spent the rest of the ride in very pleasant silence.

So, there are *taxistas* and there are *taxistas*. But on the whole, I love the river of amiable, chatty, and well-informed men who have carried me around the city day after day and week after week. When I was a reporter, I never wasted a cab ride. I'd always give the address and, in the next breath, ask his opinion of the bill I'd just learned about or the politician I'd just interviewed. I was rewarded with seas of information, some questionable but most very useful, about corruption, dalliances, promises unfulfilled. I heard just about every opinion under the sun, but almost always with the same basic yearning for a safer, fairer, cleaner Costa Rica—with, of course, better roads.

As the years went on, the conversations got a bit more personal, as if the taxi drivers who were shuttling me were a single person I was getting to know over time, and not hundreds of different men. Maybe I was feeling more comfortable in my new home; maybe the years in Costa Rica were slowly loosening my reticent Yankee tongue. Regardless, I usually learned much more than I told. Late-night rides are conducive to confessionals, and the shared pain of a rush-hour odyssey can make fast friends of anyone. I had surprising chats about love, parenthood, infertility, adoption, divorce, death. One man told me how he came home one night to find all of his belongings on fire in the street. Another, as we listened to Puccini, told me about his lifelong dream to visit the Metropolitan Opera House in New York.

Most of all, I learned about language. Showing admiration for one turn of phrase was a sure way to elicit a deluge of instruction. One man waxed poetic about his wife, and asked whether I had found my *media naranja*—my half-orange. I could infer what this meant, and was charmed. I instantly pictured two half-oranges rolling around the street, looking for each other, straight out of

Plato. This was around the time your dad and I were planning our wedding, I think, and I was in a romantic frame of mind. "I love that," I said. "How else do Costa Ricans talk about love?"

A half-hour later, I'd heard about everything from "the light of my eyes," to "the sun of my spring," to *tal pa' cual* (this for that—kind of like "two peas in a pod"), to my all-time favorite: *la horma de mi zapato. Horma* is the figure a shoemaker uses to shape or reshape a shoe. It's a way of saying you've found your perfect fit, but I also love the idea of a shoe coming home, bedraggled and misshapen, and draping itself over a nice sturdy wooden shoe tree like the ones my dad used to use. That's marriage for you: sometimes you're the bedraggled old shoe, and sometimes you're the sturdy shoe tree, and you try to avoid both being the old shoe at the same time.

That evening, as I got ready to head home from work, I realized with a curse that I'd left my frumpy walking shoes in that man's taxi. They were too old and cheap to warrant calling the cooperative and tracking down the driver, but it meant that I wouldn't be able to walk all the way home from work, since I could no more make that trek in my heels than I could fly. I had an outrageously annoying commute home that night, hobbling in my office shoes through the rain, sitting on a series of humid buses, then plunging into a giant puddle when I finally reached my neighborhood. I felt low, lonely, and homesick, as I do whenever San José shows me its claws.

I walked up to our garden gate, opened it and went in. There, bedraggled and misshapen, were my walking shoes. Clearly, the taxi driver had found them at some point in the day, realized that only one woman in his daily labors could possibly be gigantic enough to wear such boats, remembered my address, came by and tossed them over the fence, with enough skill to make them land under our outdoor table so they wouldn't get too wet in the rain.

All I could think was: *la horma de mi zapato.*

The form that shapes and reshapes us can be a partner, a child, a parent, a friend. It can be a whole country. It can be a kindly confederacy of taxi drivers, whose wit and wisdom can salvage the grumpiest day.

December 31, 2007

When the year ends in San José, women cry in the old neighborhood. The midnight countdown on Radio Reloj *launches a torrent of sobs among Adrián's relatives, gathered in his mother's front yard. They hug and weep over everything that happened during the past year, the arrivals and the losses, everything yet to come.*

I've seen this several times now, and love the New Year's tradition of heading out into the streets at midnight to greet friends and neighbors or even step into their houses for a bite, but tonight I sat in their midst, feeling strange. Nothing is new, but all of it is mine in a new way.

Our wedding ceremony over Christmas was snowy and quick at my mother's church in Maine, my mother herself officiating, and just a handful of my parents' good friends in attendance, since I have none in the area. It was everything I wanted: all I had to do was eat breakfast (toast), put on a sweater (white), and get myself to the church on time. Adrián wore my dad's overcoat and grinned when he saw the cake my parents had arranged: it said Pura Vida.

Tonight I twisted my ring on my finger and felt suddenly shy. Then a crackling old song came on the radio, couples started to dance, and Adrián's mother emerged from the crowd and put a long black wig on my head; she was wearing a pink one, just because. I found a cold Imperial as a new round of fireworks filled the street with smoke. 2008 had begun.

UN GRANITO DE ARENA

WHEN THE HONEYMOON ENDS

Dear E,

Your dad and I sat next to a moonlit pool and had a depressing conversation. As you slept peacefully in the *cabina* just behind us, we sipped our beers and watched a midnight rainstorm move in through restless palms. I confessed to him that I didn't really feel the same passion, couldn't see what I once saw, had entered a bit of a slump, was even dreaming of others.

I wasn't talking about him. I was talking about Costa Rica. Still, I felt almost as guilty as if it were our actual marriage on the line, not my marriage to his country—and your country, too.

This was a strange position in which to find myself: I love Costa Rica, and there are few things I dislike more than listening to people who have chosen to live here sit around and complain as if it had been inflicted upon them. I dislike this so much that I cannot even bring myself to list the things that were getting me down. Let's just say that it was the usual bureaucratic frustrations, the wet-footed San José schlepping, the little inconveniences. They sounded silly coming out of my mouth, and no one of them would ever be worth relocating for—but when I added them up, they contributed to a certain fatigue.

I have lived in the same house for more than ten years, but I have traveled quite a distance in that time. I have trouble channeling the college student who devoured the country with a ridiculous grin, unable to believe her good fortune, staring in rapture out of bus windows, listening wide-eyed to howler monkeys at night and thinking they were lions, making bioluminescent footprints on a deserted beach. Somewhere along the way I moved from "Will you LOOK at THIS?" to "Oh, yeah—that's amazing, isn't it?" My tone of voice is more like my New York friends' when I visit their city: "Yeah, I guess the subway *is* an incredible feat of engineering. Yeah, Central Park *is* huge. Yeah, there sure *are* a lot of Original Ray's."

It was more than just familiarity that bred contempt. The country I had gotten to know so superficially in the year 2000 has also changed a bit: its layout, its traffic, but also, I'd argue, its mood. I've told you about the time, during that newspaper internship, that I met my first Costa Rican president. ("The president of the newspaper?" my mom asked me later on the phone. "The president of the country!" I responded proudly, telling the first of many Forrest Gump-like stories I'd have for her in the years to come: the time I interviewed Martin Luther King III, the time I watched Ricky Martin jump into a helicopter at Casa Presidencial, the time I ate dinner in thrilling proximity to the Prince of Asturias, this weird gringa bumbling into fantastic situations.) The event he was attending was held in the middle of a field, and all I could think was: Where's the security? Where are the snipers? You mean anyone can just walk up to him and say hello? It was all part of my falling in love with what seemed to be Costa Rica's lighthearted, simple, peaceful way of life.

The next time I met him, I was a reporter and he was one of the two ex-presidents accused of involvement in a complex chain of kickbacks. It was a depressing time, a cynical time, even though I am sure many Costa Ricans look back on it in a positive light as a moment when tolerance for government corruption turned a corner. For me, though, those scandals happened to break at the same time that I was trudging through my first San José slums, standing in my first very long bank lines, and confronting my first bureaucratic inanities. I was noticing the trash and pollution, the inequality. I was hearing a brisk critique of Costa Rican culture and family life from my Nicaraguan housemates. I wondered, "Where am I?"

I was in Costa Rica: a real country, not a tourist destination. A place far more complicated, interesting, and sometimes hard to handle than I had ever imagined.

The Indian-American writer Jhumpa Lahiri, who writes about immigration so beautifully, went to live in Rome with her family for a while. She spoke with *The Financial Times* about the experience: "Here, I have felt free and invisible, and have felt that sense that there's another mountain to climb, I'm at the bottom of it, and that's the great challenge." Her words went right to my heart, because I recognized but didn't feel her excitement. We live abroad because we want a mountain to climb, and sometimes that mountain can seem too much for us. We want a nice flat meadow and the comforts of home.

This was more or less what I tried to explain by the pool that night. Your dad, my finest adviser, thought for a moment as the rain came down in earnest, and then offered some suggestions.

"First, think about the big things Costa Rica has given you and not the little crap," he said. "And second, see if a day at the beach makes you feel better."

I laughed dismissively at that second notion, but you know what? He was right. The beach did help me: not the ocean, but the sand. *Un granito de arena*, to be precise. Like some other phrases in this book, it's not specifically Costa Rican, but the expression, especially with the diminutive on the end of "*grano*," is oh-so-Tico to me. After all, this is a country so enamored of diminutives that its habit of changing "*-tito*" to "*-tico*" (*momentico, chiquitico*) gave its people their nickname.

It's a country where, from birth, you and all Costa Rican children were enveloped in a happy cloud of little terms. You are our *gorditos* and *muñequitas* and *bodoquitos* and *frijolitos* and *chiquitines* and *princesitas*.

It's a country where it makes perfect sense that to do your part, to chip in, to help the world, you need to *poner su granito de arena*. You set down, not a brick or a stone, but one little grain of sand at a time.

I thought about this as I compressed millions of grains of sand underneath my feet and ran along the foamy edge of low tide, an activity with an amazing power to restore sanity. I thought about the *granito de arena*, and realized that while I tend to see my relationship with Costa Rica as a marriage of sorts, there is at least one big difference between such a marriage and an actual one.

In a happy marriage between people, any desire to mold and change and push one's partner should be far outweighed, or even completely eclipsed, by acceptance. A good relationship with a country, however, needs its share of dissatisfaction. We are meant to see room for improvement and take action. We are meant to push and prod. We are meant to throw up our hands at times and swear at the newspaper, to get frustrated, to take it personally, even to mourn.

The true question for a traveler, for those with the tremendous luxury of choosing our surroundings, isn't whether the mountain is big and tiring, but whether it is ours to climb. It's not whether there are problems or there aren't—there always will be—but whether they are our problems to solve. The answer to this question is a moving target. There are days when I feel hopeful about Costa Rica and the role I can play in it, and days when I feel disheartened, just as there are days when I feel hopeful or hopeless about the future of the United States. But just figuring out the right question to ask made me feel infinitely better.

Like all parents, I want to find for myself, and for you, the best quality of life I can, but part of my quality of life is having the power to make a difference. Part of your quality of life is the chance to see your parents fighting the good fight. Part of what a country gives or denies us is traction, leverage, a voice, a place to put our little grain of sand. In that sense, and in many others, Costa Rica has never failed me.

Five riders on horseback came toward me. Even at a distance, I could see their broad smiles as they looked at the wide, empty beach, the crashing waves, the waving palms. They couldn't believe their good fortune.

I smiled back and looked past them, indecisive. There was an estuary a little ways ahead that makes a nice stopping point, but I knew you and your dad were waiting for me at our little *cabina*. I would be back soon enough, maybe next month. I would see it then.

For now, it was time to go home.

May 3, 2011

I feel like a pincushion, and this is just Infertility 101. So many women go through much worse, but I don't understand how. Just this—the years of constant trips to the doctor, the motorcycle messenger from the pharmacy arriving at my office with my injections on ice, performing the injections on myself in a bathroom stall—is about all I can handle.

The worst part is the Wall of Babies. My doctor has delivered scores over the years, and grateful parents have given him pictures that his secretary pins up on the bulletin boards covering every inch of his waiting room. To an infertile woman, this is torture, especially considering that the doctor is in demand and I generally have to wait for my frequent appointments. I stare down those babies, learning them by heart. There are a few I love and yearn for, despite myself. There are others I have come to hate: their stupid names, their ridiculous portraits. I stare them down, day after day, week after week.

Adrián is patient and kind in the face of my temper; he needs to be. I am not sure how far down this path I will be able to go. IVF is illegal in Costa Rica, and couples that reach that point have to travel to Panama for their procedures. Am I strong enough for all of that? If I'm not strong enough for that, am I strong enough for parenthood? Then again, is anyone?

IVIENDO ARRIMAO
THE CURE FOR HOMESICKNESS

Dear E,

On my first solo trip to the beach in Costa Rica, I managed to get my shoes stolen, then sold back to me. Yes, that's right. I left them under a large palm leaf so I could run barefoot, came back to find them gone, and promptly heard a cheerful bike bell as a ropy man approached me with my sneakers tucked neatly in his basket.

"Only twenty dollars," he said.

"But—but—you just stole those from me!" I protested.

His face filled with the shocked indignation of the righteous. "Stole them?" he sputtered. "I bought them from a man just now on the main street. They're practically brand new!"

That part was true, and they had cost me seventy-five dollars. They were also the only footwear I had brought with me on the trip. I looked to the left, looked to the right. It was still early and there was no one else in sight. I sighed and started to negotiate.

"Mom," you'll say here. "You *paid* him?"

Yup, ten dollars.

"Where was this?"

Jacó.

"JACÓ?" Here you'll burst into merciless laughter because, at the time of this writing, Jacó is a place where you wouldn't leave a day-old newspaper lying around without expecting its immediate and expert extraction, let alone a pair of fancy running shoes. To complete my humiliation, I'll admit that before this incident even took place—that very same morning—I had actually gotten up early to watch the sunrise, since that's what northerners do when we're at the beach. As the sky slowly lightened over the ocean and the sun failed to appear, a similarly gradual enlightenment took place in my top-notch brain. I realized I was on the Pacific coast, looking west, and that the sunrise might best be contemplated on the other side of the country. This was a place I might someday visit, if I could keep my shoes in my possession.

So yes, I'm terrible with directions. And by that I mean, *más tonta que las gallinas de noche*: dumber than hens at night.

I still have days like that—well, not quite like *that*, but failures nonetheless—and that's when I feel that I'm *viviendo arrimao*, the term for that friend or neighbor who crashes on your sofa and eats your food and just won't leave. Some days I'll even say to your father, "I think Costa Rica wants me to take a hint and go away." Of course, I'm full of self-pity on such a day and begging for a rebuttal, but it's a feeling I get sometimes.

Given the sunrise fiasco, you won't be surprised to learn that it took me nearly a decade to realize the orientation of our house. I was outside with you a couple of months ago, watching the sun set beyond our gate, when it occurred to me that my favorite spot in the house, the back corner where I sit at night as you fall asleep, is also our northernmost corner. It is the place where I read you *Pat the Bunny* or *Baby Listens*, then pull out my own book, and read, and wait. From our rocking chair, I can look out over the whole quiet length of our little house. Over the sound of your noise machine, just enough to mask throaty motorcycle engines and loudmouthed neighbors, I can still hear the crickets outside or, one evening during Lent, a somewhat tone-deaf but oddly beautiful chorus of old ladies at the stations of the cross I'd seen them putting up earlier in the day, their dutiful sons and husbands following the women's orders as usual in the gated porches and entryways of our neighborhood.

I sit like this until you're fast asleep, eyelashes lushly curved against your cheek, hands curled. Some nights, it's not that simple (look in the index under "crankiness," "*Keeping Up With the Kardashians* reruns," "begging," or "maniacal laughter"), but when it is, it's the most peaceful, quiet, and happy moment of my day, my week, my life.

So I was thrilled to discover that when I sit in that rocking chair, I am at the northernmost point of our house, looking south. It makes sense. It means I'm sitting as close as I possibly can to the place I'm from. I sit as close as I can to long, shadowed summer evenings punctuated by the far-off sound of tennis ball thwacks, to bare feet on cedar chips in my mother's garden where I fill my outstretched T-shirt with arugula and butter beans. I sit as close as I can to autumn, crisp leaves on top and muddy below, scuffed-up old Bean boots my thrifty father keeps resoling. I sit as close as I can to winter: to red, numb legs after a run; to dark mornings that I don't miss in the least; to muted heather sunsets that I miss terribly. I sit as close as I can to spring, to the joy of the first bare leg and the first sandal, even when you realize halfway out the door that you jumped the gun and are freezing cold.

I sit as close as I can to the seasons of an earlier life, seasons that now pass without me, and I feel a little *acabangada*—the Costa

Rican word for the particular melancholy of missing a person after a breakup, or an animal that has died, or a place. You can also *estar de cabanga* or, the best, *tener un cabangón*, a serious nostalgia attack that in my world would require a bottle of wine and a rainy window to gaze through.

But the *cabangón* is not for me, not tonight. No feelings of *viviendo arrimao*. I sit in the northern corner, knowing that at my back, behind the yellow curtains at the window and the sour lime tree; behind the neighbor's flower-covered wall and the streets and tin roofs beyond; behind the Nicaraguan border where ladies in frilly aprons sing about the cheeses they have to sell; behind all the borders after that, the state lines, the rivers and lakes and ocean waves of increasing frigidity; behind me, way behind me, is the life I left. But before me, to the south, is the life I came to find. Before me is the land where the streets have no name or logical layout, where rain falls in sheets, where MacGyver is a noun used in daily conversation, and where I have so often found myself as happy as can be.

All of that surrounds us, the lives behind and before us, and then they fade into the background. For right now, the only latitude and longitude that matter are the degree, minute, second, and circle of lamplight that hold the two of us together. That's why I linger so long. That's why I take my time setting you down. I want to delay the moment when thought resumes. I want to delay the moment when the lamp goes out. I want to delay the moment when the rocking chair creaks goodnight as I rise, the northern corner empties, the bedroom door closes, my feet take me back into the world, and the world begins to move once more.

June 10, 2011

First week post-op. When we found out I would need a month to recover, we turned the back bedroom into a bit of a sanctuary. We have been hoping to make it the baby's room, with a white crib and a cozy lamp and a rocking chair, and I tell myself that one day soon, we will. The doctor says this fibroid removal should help, and then a month at home, and then five more months of taking it easy, and then we'll see.

This little room was mine when I first moved in, six years ago now, back when I had two roommates and this was just a temporary landing place. Now that Adrián and I sleep in the larger front room, this one has been mostly unused for years. For this month, however, it's my place to sit and watch the rain come down.

It is a strange thing, to drop out of your life for a month. I have always thought of myself as a pretty laid-back person, and certainly of Costa Rica as a laid-back place, but being this weak and exhausted has opened my eyes. I never realized how little time I spend just sitting, just lying, just looking. I have watched approximately 13 episodes of Desperate Housewives, *brought over by a kindly coworker, but even that is pretty tiring. It is nice to sit alone and write, but that is tiring too. Mostly I have been sitting in this back corner next to the nice yellow curtains we put up, and looking out at the sour lime tree. What's funny is, I think I am going to miss this. Mostly, though, I hope it works.*

WHAT COSTA RICA TAUGHT ME ABOUT MOTHERHOOD
WHETHER I LIKE IT OR NOT *

Dear E,

To have a child in another country is to take on an entire nation as your mother-in-law. The new culture into which you've married, which once accepted you without much comment, now has plenty to say about your every move. At least, it's like that in Costa Rica, where the usual level of advice-giving bestowed upon a new mother reaches epic proportions. My actual mother-in-law, your grandmother, is very relaxed and has never given me any unsolicited parenting advice whatsoever, now that I think of it. Of course, she doesn't need to, because cashiers, waitresses, random passersby,

* Or: There really aren't any words in Spanish that start with "w."

and even our neighborhood drunk have been more than happy to instruct me.

I'm not complaining—not much, anyway—because this interference goes hand-in-hand with unbelievable kindness and support. However, especially in the first few months of motherhood, the incessant instructions from total strangers can be a bit trying. It's also quite edifying. Here are a few things Costa Ricans have taught me about parenting. To clarify, these are lessons I've been *taught*, but not all are things I've *learned*. There's a difference. Like any mother-in-law's advice, some are gems, and others you hold at arm's length. To wit:

1. It's never too hot out to wrap your baby head-to-toe in another fleece blanket.

I knew this one was coming years before I became a mother. I was out running on a scorching day, sweat pouring not only from my forehead but from every inch of skin on every person I passed, when I spotted a tiny baby wearing thick woolen pajamas, mittens, bunny slippers, and a Russian ushanka-style hat with ear flaps. I'm dead serious. Why more babies aren't hospitalized for heat exhaustion, I don't know. I've been reprimanded for insufficiently clothing you more times than I can count, including earlier today on a muggy bus where we were all fanning ourselves desperately and you, my dear, were very sensibly clad in a sleeveless cotton dress. The woman next to me commented on the extreme heat, mentioned that you looked hot as well, and then asked, "But that's all you put her in? Aren't you worried she'll catch a cold?" At which point I whipped out an ushanka and blanketed your ears in fur. All right, I didn't, but I think that would have been the only acceptable response.

2. Chamomile tea solves everything.

This is one I've taken on board wholeheartedly. In fact, it's strange to think that there was a time in my life when I didn't think of chamomile tea in almost any situation, for babies or adults. Gas or colic? A little tea in the bottle, and more for mom. Heading off for vaccinations? Put some washcloths in a jar of tea in the fridge so they're nice and cool to reduce swelling afterwards. Teething? Rub a special chamomile powder directly on the gums. Bump on the head? Stressful day? Heart attack in the works? Everything's better with a little *té de manzanilla*. It represents a broader characteristic of Costa Rica that I admire tremendously—an affection for simple, plant-based cures, not because they're trendy, but because they're cheap and effective.

3. Baby carriers are unnecessary torture devices.

I love my trusty, simple, canvas baby carrier, and so do you, little girl. It's allowed us to get around San José without a car for many months, hopping in and out of buses with the greatest of ease, striding over damaged and holey sidewalks that would derail a stroller. It's easy to protect with a single umbrella, and perfect for your nap on a fussy day.

They are gaining in popularity among Costa Rican mothers by the hour, but to many people, older women in particular, they are still an alien device. I've received many unfriendly stares and comments such as, "Poor thing. I supposed she's used to that contraption"—this as you're peacefully sleeping or joyfully bouncing up and down. There's a good reason for this, however. In Costa Rica, parents are used to simply carrying their babies in their arms. Imagine that!

A good friend in the States told me a story about a fellow mom who'd left her car seat at home, or something, and couldn't figure out how to get her baby along a sidewalk from point A to point B. My friend said, "In your arms, perhaps?" and was met with astonishment. Back in the US of A, we like to have equipment for everything, duly JPMA-certified and with an instruction manual the size of the Old Testament. In Costa Rica, this madness has simply not set in, partly for economic reasons and partly for cultural ones. That doesn't mean I no longer get nervous watching a mother leap off of a rickety, steep bus staircase onto a crumbling curb while rocking mile-high stilettos, all with a week-old baby cradled in the crook of her arm. I think there's a happy medium to be sought here.

4. Get over yourself with your organic quinoa baby food and five-point high-chair harnesses.

When I was preparing for your arrival, I was reading the same articles and scouring the same websites as any U.S. mother, but in a country with nowhere near the same range of products to buy. I worried that I wasn't going to be able to get you the right things, that you'd be unsafe and filled with chemicals and so on and so forth. The Costa Rican side of the family tended to greet my concerns with calm, compassionate smiles and not much else. I came to realize what was behind those smiles: the knowledge that babies really don't require as much stuff, or information, as overly connected new moms tend to seek out. I'm not knocking organic food or quinoa or five-point harnesses. I'm knocking the level of stress that, from what I can see, surrounds so much of U.S. babyhood, at least for people with the time and economic means for such things. That said . . .

5. Every culture gets silly about babies in its own way.

This is the most important thing I've learned, and it's why I believe any parent, from any country, would benefit from living or traveling abroad. It might sound trite to say that there's no correct way to raise a child, but receiving parenting advice from more than one culture really drives that home. Costa Ricans go overboard wrapping their babies in wool on sweltering days, just as people in the States are obsessed with having a specific piece of baby equipment for every conceivable occasion. A Costa Rican mother might run around town with her baby in her arms, while a gringa might be more relaxed about letting her baby play in the dirt. It's all summed up by the common phrase *"cada loco con su tema,"* another favorite of your father's—every nut has his own pet subject. It's especially true for parents, who are crazy with love.

I think the answer is to learn from each other's oddities and obsessions: the Tica mother taking off that extra sweater, the gringa carrying her baby to her neighbor's in her arms. The key is to remember that the reason we're so nuts is that we want our kids to be okay. We must teach each other the one thing that almost any parent needs to learn, and learn, and learn again: that really, all of us are making it up as we go.

December 5, 2011

We had been waiting to be parents for so long that when pregnancy finally came, we got used to the idea instantly. I talked to our baby, wrote to our baby, sang to our baby as I walked to and from work. The loss is almost unbearable. I say "almost" because I'm still here, aren't I? But I kind of wish I weren't.

It is a common story, told in just a few words, short and bitter, rhythmic like the heartbeat that wasn't there: Ultrasound. Doctor's sigh. Nothingness. Darkness. Heartbreak. A few days of tests and agonizing uncertainty, although deep down we already knew. On Thanksgiving Day, my parents' anniversary, we found out for sure.

Then: getting my body to let go. Drugs that left me writhing on our living room floor. I managed to make a joke on the phone to my mother, a joke that wasn't really a joke—if I've taken so many drugs to get pregnant, isn't it unfair that I should have to take drugs that achieve the opposite? They didn't work, either, and a procedure at the hospital followed. I crossed that familiar sidewalk with a ghost in my belly and left feeling like a ghost myself.

I don't want to get up, or to stay in bed; I don't want to watch or read anything, but I don't want to sit in silence, either. The next-door kids gathered yesterday in our garden to chat, not realizing anyone was home. I snapped at them like an old witch and raged at their languid, teenage drifting-away.

The only good thing I can say is that I love my husband in a way I didn't know was possible. Shared joy is one thing, but shared grief, when no one else on the whole planet was a part of this particular life . . . That day when we got off the phone, our bed became the only place in the universe. A horrible place to be, and the only place I wanted to be.

You know what? I don't want to write, either, so that's it for now.

XIOMARA KIMBERLING HAMLET STEVE

THE JOY OF NAMES

Dear E,

The Christmas season in Costa Rica is an embarrassment of riches. Where I come from, Christmas is a bright and festive light in the middle of the cold and dark—and that has its own, unparalleled beauty. Here, however, it's everything good all at once: The rainy season is over and summer is here, with its sunny days and cool Christmas winds! School's out! The *aguinaldo* has arrived! Tax season is ending, time off is approaching, the streets and shops are full of lights, there are tamales and *rompope* and Tapitas Navideñas everywhere! Quick, someone get me some more exclamation points! It's overwhelming, in the best possible way, like a fantasy. I can't even imagine what it's like for kids. I wonder if there's a spike in hyperventilation rates at the Children's Hospital.

By the way, small one, if you're reading this all grown up in a place that involves earmuffs and antifreeze, I know you just said, "You can take your 'embarrassment of riches' and stick it in a place where the sun don't shine. As in, the place where I live." I can hear you from here. But while I know from long experience that the rainy season doesn't compare to a long, hard winter, it really is a whole lotta water, and the start of the dry season carries some of the same feeling of those precious first days of spring up north. Walking around without an umbrella on early December afternoons gives you that same sensation of being sprung from a cage, of being out after curfew. You want to run and dance or sing, and do everything outside, and sit out on patios with rows of cold beers.

During the Christmas season just before you were born, your dad and I spent those afternoons discussing names: yours, to be exact. Deciding on it was a difficult task, primarily because your dad must have been a horrible elementary school classmate. He has an uncanny ability to find the rude words that rhyme with a name, and did so mercilessly as I read entries in the baby-name book out loud. He then discarded most of the rest as old-fashioned or weird, and I discarded any that would be notably different in English and Spanish, and by the time we were done, well—it's a miracle your name isn't You-yeah-you-over-there.

Behind the names we finally chose for you, however, were a sea of names on another list we began well before we even wanted to be parents. These were names we wouldn't choose for our own child, but that we collected and curated like works of art. Some came from the voting lists I perused—first idly, then with increasing delight—as I stood outside the elementary school in the neighborhood where your dad grew up, waiting as he voted for president inside. I discovered a "Kimberling," apparently male, and stored the name away for our list. Some were historic: there were Costa Rican kids named "Welcome Kennedy" after JFK's visit to the country, and others named Nixon or Stalin. Others were the names of kids my friends came across, such as "Eskywalker" or "Maybe." Still others came from the occasional publications in national papers of the most unusual names from the year before: "Hamlet Steve" was one of those, as was "Alien Gerardo." Discovering odd names became a shared passion. Trust me, kid. You're lucky.

But names of individuals are just the beginning. On another gorgeous December afternoon years ago, I sat with your dad and his mother, your "Mima," on her front porch. It was one of the best afternoons I've spent in Costa Rica. All we did was drink our coffee, watch the world go by, enjoy the sun, and chat. And by "chat," I mean that they told me all about how Costa Rican family nicknames work.

One of them was telling a story and referred to "*las panaderas*" (the bakers, female). I was confused, and they explained that since the mother is a baker, the whole family—mother and daughters—is known by that name. I asked, "Are there any other nicknames in the neighborhood?" And for the next hour or so, they came up with about 40 different names as I took copious notes. It turned out that every single home in the neighborhood had a special nickname floating above its roof, visible only to insiders. No wonder I had never understood directions around here. "You can't miss it! Just go down by the Crazies' house, turn left and keep going until you hit the Fish Sticks."

The whole business of nicknames in Costa Rica is a complex affair, but the family nicknames have a special place in my heart. In the United States, at least in the places I have lived, we had a certain neighborhood shorthand, but nothing like this. I won't list the names I wrote down that day because I want to make sure your Costa Rican relatives don't have to move, but some of the ones I've heard and read over the subsequent years include:

- Nicknames based on physical characteristics. "*Los cepillo*" is a family whose dad has sticky-up hair like a brush, or "*Los pan dulce*" could be so named because the matriarch wears her hair pulled back into the shape of a sweet roll. These two cases, as it has been explained to me, mix plural and singular—"*los*" and "*cepillo*"—because while they describe a group, only one member of the family has the characteristic. See below.
- Nicknames generalized to the whole family because of the nickname of one member, usually the dad. A man known as "*Pollo*" is of course the father of the family known as "The Chickens."

• Nicknames based on professions. "The Bakers" falls into this category, or "The Carriage-Drivers," which must either refer to taxi drivers or go way back.

• Nicknames based on personality or old neighborhood lore. "The Crazies" is such an example.

• Or, always my favorites, tons and tons of nicknames no one can seem to explain. Why "The Jars"? No idea. Did it have something to do with a story with the brother way back? No, we can't remember. "The Sausages"? Who knows?

A conversation about these things is better than poring over a photo album. You hear the stories, the rumors, the unanswered questions. Uncle so-and-so or cousin *tal fulano* is called in to clarify just why that one guy whose actual name no one can remember earned the nickname of "The Bedcovers" for his entire family.

Of course, nicknames must be used with care. They can create a sense of jovial familiarity, but they can also be problematic. I can honestly say that I have never heard a racist neighborhood nickname being used (or at least, one I recognized as such), but they must exist. A person who is alcoholic or addicted to drugs can earn a corresponding nickname for his or her entire family, thus codifying the already difficult legacy that the children have to bear. And while it's one thing to make fun of a family's unruly hair, there are nicknames that turn much more unfortunate physical characteristics into the butt of jokes.

I love living in a neighborhood of Parrots and Tarzans rather than Joneses and Smiths, but it's certainly incumbent on all of us—as neighbors, and especially as parents—to sort through these issues with sensitivity, seeking that sweet spot before humor becomes cruelty. Is this a nickname I would say to their faces? Or, more importantly, in front of the children? This is a judgment call every culture, maybe even every neighborhood, must make for itself, because standards are different in different places. Costa Rica is, without any doubt, much more open about pointing out all kinds of physical characteristics than we were in my own upbringing. If you're fat, people will call you fat; it's not a big secret, nor is it taboo. If you're skinny as a rail, people will call you a flat board or say that you're doing a handstand: that is, your legs are so skinny they look like arms. As a person who has always struggled with weight, I find this refreshing and even liberating, but mine is only one experience. This is complicated, especially when it comes to race or ethnicity, for example.

As the sun set on that early December day, at the end of the recounting of neighborhood stories and jokes, I asked your dad and grandmother, "And what is your family called?" There was a thoughtful, surprised silence. It was obvious that this question had never before been posed. "Are you serious? A list the length of my arm, and you don't know what everyone calls YOU?"

They really didn't. I found this both fascinating and mysterious, and I eventually got to the bottom of it. They are "The Sweet Rolls" mentioned above. At least, that's the version I was given.

What are we called, you might ask? I can't be sure, but I have a hunch, based on the way you saunter around the block, the way you illuminate the faces of the neighbors who see you, neighbors who never before gave me the time of day (nor I them, to be fair). If anyone on our street has something to say about your dad or me, I know exactly how they phrase it. I know it because I've heard people refer to our house as "*donde Emma*"—where Emma lives.

We are "*los de Emma.*" And we are. We're all yours.

September 10, 2012

She is coming she is coming she is coming.

Called my parents from the street outside our doctor's office to tell them we are having a girl. My mom is the only one who knew from the start. Everyone else has predicted a boy, including the woman who cleans our office at Casa Presidencial.

Later, at work, I told that woman my news.

"I knew it," she said. "I told you. I knew it was a girl because of your sad eyes."

I usually suffer from over-niceness, but I was not about to let that one slide.

"No, you said it was a boy. And my eyes are not sad. I can guarantee you, of all the women on the face of this earth, I am the one with happy eyes."

"Well," she said, "gracias a Dios," and off she went, sweeping.

DIJO A CORRER!
INDEPENDENCE

Dear E,

Three years ago tonight, I felt you kick for the very first time. I was standing on the corner of our street, watching the kids walk by with their *faroles*, tiny dots of light in the darkness. As if you were stirred by all the kids milling around you, I felt the smallest of bubbles somewhere within: pop pop pop. I'm here. It wasn't until hours later that I was sure what I was feeling, but I felt it on that corner on the eve of Independence Day.

The *faroles* are a Costa Rican homage to the lanterns women carried in Guatemala, this night in 1821, as they waited outside the Palacio del Gobierno to find out whether the men huddled within would put an end to 300 years of Spanish rule. Independence took nearly a month to reach Costa Rica—the vote here was held on Oct. 11 of that year—but September 14th is the night when Costa Rican kids take paper lanterns and march through the streets. It's always been one of my favorite Costa Rican traditions, although now, thanks to you, I have a real ticket to the show.

Your own independence won't be won overnight, although I know it will feel that way to me. It does already. Tonight we walked around the corner to the neighborhood school and into a noisy crowd of kids and parents, with a warbling, unintelligible teacher's voice barely audible from somewhere in the building's innards. A vast city and menagerie of lanterns circled us, store-bought and homemade, depicting houses, *pulperías*, turtles, toucans, Celso Borges' soccer jersey. Cars whizzed past and we wondered how this sea of small humans was supposed to launch forth into the traffic, but then a man emerged with a very large flashlight and megaphone, the universal signals of tremendous authority, and motioned us forward.

The school band of xylophones and drums played, for some reason, "When the Saints Go Marching In." Your dad addressed you in English. I addressed you in Spanish. In that slush of languages and cultures, we plunged into the street.

You had clung to my legs at the school, overwhelmed by the huge mob of restless kids and tired parents, and once the parade began you assessed the scene for about half a block. Then, however, you discovered you were in your element. Walking. Lights. Interesting noises. Need I say more?

"Look at all the PEOPLE," you said with deep delight.

"Yup. These are your people," I responded.

You took this rather literally. "Come on!" you said to the crowd around you in a commanding tone, marching forward, holding your flashing LED light in your hand—the lantern we'd brought had proved too unwieldy for you. "Awwww, YEAH."

Y dijo a correr. Literally, "S/he said, 'Let's run!'" This construction—*y dijo a correr, y dijo a llorar, y dijo a comer*—denotes bursting, jumping, flying into action. You took off running. Not walking, but running in the dark.

This little creature who, three years ago tonight, had just that moment begun to make herself felt within her mother's belly, was ready to storm the barricades. You sprinted ahead happily, savoring your freedom. Your dad and I walked behind you in the crowd, our eyes always fixed on the pigtails in front of us, little glints of gold in the dark. We held hands in the fleeting way of the parents of toddlers: catching each other for a few moments, then releasing as one or the other lunged forward to keep you from moving too far away in the throng, or to make sure you wouldn't fall into a gutter deeper than you are tall. What I have learned about marriage-while-parenting thus far is that if the two parents can keep their hands coming back together, the way tennis players should reset to the center after every stroke, that's a beginning.

We watched you revel in your first nighttime parade, an early taste of independence. We watched, conscious that you will take on the world many times in the years ahead, and that we must enjoy these front-row seats while we can. We watched, knowing that our own independence will never be quite the same, we chaperones whose eyes were glued to you, we followers who mirrored your movements left or right, forward or back. We are no longer sovereign states. We have been conquered, fair and square, but that's just what we'd been hoping for. We surrendered long ago with open arms.

My last workday of the year ended with a meeting near La Sabana on the west side of town, and I decided to walk all the way east to the San Pedro bus stop. A long trek, but at seven months pregnant, I feel like I could conquer the world.

It was a lovely afternoon, breezy and just sunny enough, and as I strode along the old daily route from my English-teaching days, the Avenida Central pedestrian boulevard, I was feeling so luxurious and free that I decided to go for a treat at the National Theater coffee shop. While I was there, a Christmas show started up outside; I watched it through the theater's tall, narrow windows.

At the end of the show, a choir performed "El Año Viejo," the ubiquitous year-end anthem that is always played at midnight on New Year's Eve. I've always loved it, because with lyrics like this, how could you not: "I won't forget the old year / because it left me very good things. / It gave me a goat / a black donkey / a white mare / and a good mother-in-law."

Tears came to my eyes as I stood there in the plaza that I'd gravitated toward in my first days in San José, where I'd sat for so many hours scribbling in my journal, outside the theater where I'd attended my first opera and my first (and probably last) state dinner. I felt my big belly, my Costa Rican baby. I am still, and always will be, an outsider, but this scene before me will be hers. This song, her New Year's tradition. This theater, her heritage. What can I say that Jhumpa Lahiri did not say already: "There are times I am bewildered by each mile I have traveled, each meal I have eaten, each person I have known, each room in which I have slept. As ordinary as it all appears, there are times when it is beyond my imagination."

When I finally headed downhill toward my bus stop, I came across one last reason to pause for awhile: a Scottish-American man, as he identified himself in broken Spanish, was standing across from Taco Bell in a kilt, entertaining his Costa Rican audience with bagpipe classics.

I had to laugh. Of course he was. Where else would he be?

Z ARPE

ONE FOR THE ROAD

Dear E,

This last word is one that most visitors learn, almost like *pura vida*. *El zarpe* is the departure of a ship from port, but it's also the sailor's last drink before climbing on board. I picture an old man in yellow waders and a cable-knit sweater, tossing one last whiskey past his grizzled beard on a gloomy Massachusetts day, but the term really belongs to a lanky fisherman with an icy beer or bottle of guaro in a place like Puntarenas. As you know, my dear, that's a hot, flat, narrow Pacific port town. As you might not know, it's where your father bought your mother her first *copo*, knowing that the shaved ice, sweet syrup, condensed and powdered milk would keep her from falling flat on her face at a patron saint's festival.

Why was I in danger of falling flat on my face? That's a story for another time. Or never. But I believe the medical term is "too many *zarpes*."

For landlubbers, this term helps ensure that another round of drinks will be ordered over some sensible soul's objections. You say, "Come on! *El zarpe, el zarpe!* One for the road!" The person always relents. Repeat this for five or six rounds more and you've got the correct usage, both of the term and of those nice cold bottles of beer sitting in a bucket of ice, ideally in a dimly lit bar on a rainy afternoon with the best of the '80s piping through your brain.

I've had a lot of people set sail on me in the past decade, off to other lands. Such is life, and certainly the life of the expat. When I first arrived here, I was lonely, washed up on a strange beach and watching my friends and family recede into the distance. The tide came in. My life filled with friendships, the really good kind, the ones you can only make when you're far from home and a little bit lost. Then, as the years went by, the tide went out again. One by one, or sometimes in pairs, people peeled off and headed back home, leaving me sitting on the beach once more. I'm not all alone this time, of course. I keep the greatest possible company. But I no longer have folks in my daily life for whom Enrique and Beto are really Ernie and Bert.

I'd like to say that these many departures have made me appreciate the people who are around me now, every moment of every day, but that's not always true. I don't think that's even desirable. If we really achieved that, we'd cry every time anyone left the house. (Just like you do. Hmm. Perhaps you're onto something there.) However, I have decided that the *zarpe* is not only an outstanding way to develop a drinking problem, but also a good approach to life. It encourages indulgence in pleasures because of their finite nature. We have one more with our friends because our ship, or theirs, might sail at any time. It is a jolly way of keeping in mind the fact that our time on shore, at the bar, and in life, is always limited. To me, that jovial awareness of mortality is very Costa Rican.

With you, little bean, the *zarpe* is a little bit different. Shall we squish one more of our neighbor's spectacular flowers into pulpy red mush in our hands? Ok, *el zarpe, el zarpe.* (Sorry, don Gonzalo.) Go up and down the driveway again pointing at oranges? Ok, *el zarpe, el zarpe*. Pretend your comb is a phone and stomp around naked? Go for it. No time like the present.

In this book of phrases, here's my *zarpe* for you, one more for the road: *cada cabeza es un mundo*. Every head is its own world. These words have dropped from your father's lips so many times, tiny soothing antacid pills for my latest emotional heartburn. Like Costa Rica itself, they remind me that acceptance is often the wisest path, especially when it comes to human foibles. We can fret and spin, or we can throw up our hands and shrug our shoulders, remembering that we ourselves are every bit as maddening and mysterious as anyone else.

If every head is its own world, then a couple is the strange and miraculous country that is made where two worlds overlap—the territory inside the place where the two orbs cross, the center of a Venn diagram. Every couple's country is different. It can be the most wonderful place imaginable, where the loneliness of the cold universe is forgotten, or it can be desolate and silent. It can change over time: large and expansive on exhilarating, invulnerable days, cramped and airless when times are bad. It passes through seasons, frosts and thaws, leaves that fall and grow again. It is the small sliver of our vastness that we share with another person. It is home to our giddiest nights and bleary-eyed breakfasts, bitter sighs and eyes that speak volumes. It is the place where our children are born. It is their whole universe, until they begin to venture forth beyond it.

I have learned many things during my ten years in Costa Rica, but none more important than this: love is its own country, wherever it is found. Ours, your father's and mine, is limited to the south by Panama and to the north by the stone wall at your grandparents' house in Maine. Its official languages are English and Spanish, with the regional and familial linguistic quirks that are ours alone. Its national dish is the *chicharrón*. Its national anthem would surely be the subject of fierce debate, though it's definitely by Joaquín Sabina. Its population of native-born citizens is one: you.

That might sound like a lonely proposition, but there is loneliness in simply being alive. After all, I hear that every head is its own world. As Milton put it in *Paradise Lost*, "The mind is its own place, and in itself can make a heaven of hell, a hell of heaven." May you never have to do either. May your world be full of heavenly things you take from your past and make for yourself. May you save yourself the pain that comes from believing that we can ever completely know, let alone control, another person. Whether that person is your parent or your partner, half a world away or brushing against your arm on the couch, Costa Rican, American or Azerbaijani, you will only ever know one fraction of the depths within. If that little sliver that you share is a happy place, that is enough. More than enough: it's marvelous.

February 8, 2013

Your birthday. The dividing line of my life, before and after.
The start of yours. The day you set sail.

ACKNOWLEDGEMENTS

I'm grateful, first and foremost, to *The Tico Times*. For my first three years in Costa Rica, it was the physical center of my universe, that funny little house near the Judicial Branch where some of my best friends in the world filed into a perpetually dusty newsroom every day and we had the time of our lives—not always in the newsroom itself, but in the streets and towns and jungles it sent us out to cover, and in the bars where we recovered from our arduous labors. It's still my home, but in a more amorphous way, as a website and a set of alumni around the world tied together by their love for journalism and for Costa Rica.

Thank you to all those early colleagues and friends, particularly the group of women who have stayed in touch as we became mothers, supporting each other through joy and pain over Family Pizza and, later, across many miles. Our children are Costa Rican by blood or in spirit, and they are forever united by their mothers' newsroom friendships. Rebecca, Heidi, Mónica, Meg, Gaby and Sophia: you and each of your kids have a special place in my heart for life.

Thank you, more recently, to David Boddiger for bringing me back on board and for his constant support, including with the start of the "Maeology" column; Robert Isenberg for his terrific writing and encouragement; Jill Replogle and Karl Kahler for their editing and comments on many of these texts; Andrés Madrigal for stepping up to the plate at a crucial moment; and all of my coworkers there.

So many of those colleagues went out of their way to make this book happen, two in particular. Robin Kazmier was a kind, thoughtful, thorough, and wonderfully organized editor and co-conspirator. Thank you, above all, to publisher Jonathan Harris for believing in my column and in this book. Truly, your mind-boggling personal commitment to *The Tico Times*, your generous trust and your unflagging encouragement have made a lifelong dream of mine come true. I'll be forever grateful.

That dream sprang to life before my eyes the first time I saw one of Priscilla Aguirre's illustrations and squealed with joy. When I came across her work a few years back at a booth at an art fair, I felt an instant sense of recognition and excitement: her Holalola designs capture the elements of Costa Rica I most love, and that many visitors rush past on the way to the beach. I still can't believe hers was the pen that transformed these essays into images. I am deeply indebted to her for illustrating my first years with my daughter so beautifully.

My family happens to be full of kind, voracious readers and eloquent writers who have offered constant support. To name just a few: My aunt Joan and my brother Tom share with me the immigrant experience. My father, writer of equations on placemats and wise, rambling, heartfelt emails, is the ultimate giver of advice and the voice in my head. My mother, writer of sermons, shaped me as an author more than anyone else, including as my third-grade teacher; she has been my greatest writing cheerleader ever since. And my brother John, writer of the fantastic children's book *Mickey Price: Journey to Oblivion*, showed me what's possible. A few years back, I watched from afar, jaw on the floor, as the busiest person I know woke up early on weekends to sit in a coffee shop and write, driven by his desire to cook up the ultimate yarn for his twin boys. That spirit inspired me as I started a late-night blog for my own little girl, and kept me from giving up at several points along the way.

I offer up these reflections in memory of my indomitable grandmother, Jane B. Grant, and my gutsy and unforgettable aunt, Diane K. Stanley. It was to visit Aunt Diane that I first came to Costa Rica in 1987, when she was working at the U.S. Embassy in San José. I have felt more than once that she might be watching my adventures and misadventures with a smile.

Finally, I thank my beloved Adrián and Emma Jane. So much of this book comes from him, in one way or another, as my guide through this life, my interpreter, my home; and every word on these pages is for her.

ENDNOTES

As mentioned at the beginning of the book in "A Note on Costa Rican Slang," I am generally indebted to the Costa Rican writers María Mayela Padilla and Carlos Arauz for confirming and enriching my understanding of so many Costa Rican sayings. Truly, Mr. Arauz's *Dichos y refranes costarricenses: Frases y expresiones de nuestra habla popular* (published by the author, 2008), and Ms. Padilla's *Dichos y refranes de los ticos: Un 'gallo pinto' de costarriqueñismos* (Jadine, 2013), are essential volumes for any foreign resident of Costa Rica, or anyone else fascinated by this subject.

The *Los Angeles Times* story quoted in *"Antiguo higuerón"* (p. 16) was written by Marla Dickerson and published on November 5, 2007: "With Costa Rica's mail, it's address unknown."

The information about *malespín* slang in *"Breteanding"* (p. 20) came from various sources. I initially learned of its existence through a Facebook message from a *Tico Times* reader, and found additional information in sources including the article *"El inglés y el malespín en el lenguaje pandillero,"* by Róger Matus Lazo, published by Nicaragua's La Prensa on June 5, 2005, and the article *"Tras los orígenes del 'tuani,'"* by Daisy Largaespaldas, published on the blog managuafuriosa.com on May 19, 2016.

The Pema Chödrön passage cited in *"Cafetal"* (p. 26) is from *When Things Fall Apart: Heart Advice for Difficult Times* (Shambala Publications, Inc., 2000).

The Vladimir Nabokov quotation in *"Hablando paja"* (p. 50) is from *Speak, Memory: An Autobiography Revisited,* published as *Conclu-*

sive Evidence in 1951 and reissued in 1999 by Reed Business Information, Inc.

The Sandra Cisneros quotation in *"Katerín Estalin"* (p. 63) is from her short story "Eleven," published in *Woman Hollering Creek* (Random House, 1991).

The prayer paraphrased in *"MacGyver"* (p. 77) was offered in honor of the inauguration of President Barack Obama by Episcopal Bishop Gene Robinson on January 19, 2009. "A Prayer for the Nation and Our Next President, Barack Obama" can be read at episcopalcafe.com or viewed on YouTube.

The newspaper story that gave a snapshot of one day's glacial slowness in San José as described in *"Requetefurris"* (p. 99) was written by Alvaro Murillo and published in *La Nación* on September 20, 2013: *"Crónica: recorriendo La Sabana a un kilómetro por hora."*

The interview with Jhumpa Lahiri cited in *"Un granito de arena"* (p. 119) was written by Sheila Pierce and appeared online in The Financial Times on May 22, 2015. The Lahiri quotation in the December 20, 2012 journal entry is from *Interpreter of Maladies* (Houghton Mifflin Harcourt, 1999).

Background information on the tradition of the faroles described in *"Y dijo a correr"* (p. 141) came from the article *"Faroles recordaron vigilia de una noche,"* by Michelle Soto, published online by Costa Rica's La Nación on September 15, 2015.

The Green Season
by Robert Isenberg

"The Green Season" is a dynamic collection of essays and reportage by former Tico Times staff writer Robert Isenberg, who covered arts, culture and travel for the paper from 2013 to 2015. With his trademark humor and observation, Isenberg describes the people, culture, and biodiversity that make Costa Rica so unique— from a centuries-old indigenous ceremony to a remote jungle crisscrossed by crocodile-filled canals. Isenberg explores the country head-on, fighting his way through San José traffic, mingling with venomous snakes, and even making a cameo in an epic soccer film at the height of World Cup fever. Richly detailed and tenderly written, "The Green Season" is as entertaining as it is informative.

Praise for "The Green Season":

"'The Green Season' offers a personal glimpse into the joys and frustrations of expat life in Costa Rica. Isenberg delights in capturing the country's daily rhythms, from the magical to the mundane. An honest, thoughtful look at modern-day Costa Rica."
-- James Kaiser, author of "Costa Rica: The Complete Guide"

"Robert Isenberg has a delightful way of describing the new horizons around him....Everyone he meets opens up to him and we get to infiltrate and experience new places, new cultures and new friends alongside him. I, for one, intend to read all his books.
-- Caroline Kennedy, author of
"How the English Establishment Framed Stephen Ward"

"The Green Season" is available worldwide on Amazon in paperback and e-book formats (http://amzn.to/23mcT5d), or for delivery within Costa Rica at store.ticotimes.net/collections/books.

Katherine Stanley Obando is a writer, editor, translator, speechwriter and nonprofit communications specialist. A graduate of Harvard College and a former Teach for America corps member, she moved to Costa Rica in 2004, where she has worked as a teacher, journalist and presidential adviser, and in various leadership positions within the nonprofit and education sectors. She is a co-founder of JumpStart Costa Rica, a project that provides intensive, free English camps and hands-on teacher training in low-income rural and urban areas. Katherine lives in San José with her husband and daughter.

Read more at www.katherinestanley.com.

Priscilla Aguirre is a Costa Rican artist and designer. She is the creative director and owner of the Holalola stationery and gift brand, which she created in an effort to capture Costa Rica's identity in a way that goes beyond traditional palm-tree-and-beachscape tourism imagery. Her whimsical and distinctive works have quickly become ubiquitous in the suitcases of visitors and the walls of residents nationwide. She lives in San José with her husband and son.

See more of Priscilla's work at www.holalolashop.com.

The Tico Times is Central America's most distinguished English-language newspaper, founded in 1956. It provides daily news, features, and analysis of Costa Rica. *Love in Translation: Letters to My Costa Rican Daughter* is the second book from The Tico Times Publications Group, which also published *The Green Season: A Writer's First Year in Costa Rica*, by staff writer Robert Isenberg, in 2015.

Visit us at www.ticotimes.net.

Made in the USA
Middletown, DE
25 April 2017